Safeguarding Children from Emotional Maltreatment

Safeguarding Children Across Services Series
Series editors: Carolyn Davies and Harriet Ward

Safeguarding children from abuse is of paramount importance. This series communicates messages for practice from an extensive government-funded research programme designed to improve early recognition of child abuse as well as service responses and interventions. The series addresses a range of forms of abuse, including emotional and physical abuse and neglect, and outlines strategies for effective interagency collaboration, successful intervention and best practice. Titles in the series will be essential reading for practitioners with responsibility for safeguarding children

Harriet Ward is Director of the Centre for Child and Family Research and Research Professor at Loughborough University, UK.

Carolyn Davies is Research Advisor at Thomas Coram Research Unit at Institute of Education, University of London, UK.

of related interest

Child Protection Systems in the United Kingdom
A Comparative Analysis
Anne Stafford, Nigel Parton, Sharon Vincent and Connie Smith
ISBN 978 1 84905 067 8

Safeguarding Children in Primary Health Care
Edited by Julie Taylor and Markus Themessl-Huber
ISBN 978 1 84310 652 4

Safeguarding Children Living with Trauma and Family Violence
Evidence-Based Assessment, Analysis and Planning Interventions
Arnon Bentovim, Antony Cox, Liza Bingley Miller and Stephen Pizzey
ISBN 978 1 84310 938 9

The Child's World
The Comprehensive Guide to Assessing Children in Need
2nd edition
Edited by Jan Howarth
ISBN 978 1 84310 568 8

Good Practice in Safeguarding Children
Working Effectively in Child Protection
Edited by Liz Hughes and Hilary Owen
ISBN 978 1 84310 945 7

Safeguarding Children from Emotional Maltreatment
What Works

Jane Barlow and Anita Schrader McMillan

Jessica Kingsley *Publishers*
London and Philadelphia

First published in 2010
by Jessica Kingsley Publishers
116 Pentonville Road
London N1 9JB, UK
and
400 Market Street, Suite 400
Philadelphia, PA 19106, USA

www.jkp.com

Copyright © Jane Barlow and Anita Schrader McMillan 2010
Printed digitally since 2012

Library of Congress Cataloging in Publication Data
Barlow, Jane, 1962-
  Safeguarding children from emotional maltreatment : what works / Jane Barlow and Anita
Schrader McMillan.
      p. cm.
  Includes bibliographical references and index.
  ISBN 978-1-84905-053-1 (alk. paper)
  1. Psychological child abuse--Prevention. 2. Problem families. I. McMillan, Anita Schrader.
II. Title.
  RC569.5.P75B37 2010
  616.85'82--dc22

British Library Cataloguing in Publication Data
A CIP catalogue record for this book is available from the British Library

ISBN 978 1 84905 053 1

Contents

Acknowledgements

We would like to extend our thanks to the Department for Children, Schools and Families and the Department of Health for their support in overseeing this study, particularly Carolyn Davies, Jenny Gray, Isabella Craig, Christine Humphrey and Zoltan Bozoky.

Thanks are also due to the following members of Warwick Medical School who were joint applicants on the original grant and for their expert guidance and comments on the final report as members of the steering group: Yvonne Carter, Moli Paul, Peter Sidebotham and Sarah Stewart-Brown. We are also very grateful to David Jones and Paul Ramchandani for their guidance in the reformulation of the original report into a final publication, and to Professor Hilton Davis and Dr Danya Glaser for their comments on the final publication.

The views expressed in this report are the authors' and do not necessarily reflect those of the Department for Children, Schools and Families and the Department of Health.

Section One

Emotional Maltreatment and its Consequences

1

Introduction

'Emotional abuse does not leave physical injuries and its ongoing nature usually means there is no crisis which would precipitate its identification by the health, welfare or criminal justice systems'. As a consequence, it is the most hidden and underestimated form of child maltreatment.' (Evans 2002)

Background

Emotional maltreatment is an inadequately researched and poorly understood concept despite increasing awareness about its critical effect on children's happiness and wellbeing. As many as 80 per cent of children who have experienced physical abuse and neglect have also experienced emotional abuse and it has been suggested that it unifies and underpins all types of maltreatment, and that the emotional dimension of maltreatment is central to an understanding of all abuse and neglect (Glaser and Prior 2002). However, it also occurs on its own, and in 1980 it was introduced as a criterion for inclusion on child protection registers in England and Wales. During the last ten years the number and percentage of children on the child protection register who were registered for primary emotional abuse rose significantly. Prevalence studies in the UK and elsewhere, however, suggest that registered cases of emotional abuse represent just the tip of the iceberg, and that children who are now subject to a child protection plan comprise only a small proportion of the total number of children actually experiencing abuse of this type (see Chapter 2).

Increased concern about emotional maltreatment has given rise to an increase in interest in how best to 'treat' it, and it has been suggested that 'no other form of child abuse has created so many difficulties for practitioners and so much confusion for researchers and theorists alike' (Iwaniec 1995). In 2008 the Department for Children, Schools and Families and the Department of Health commissioned a series of projects as part of the

'Safeguarding Children' Research Initiative to examine its causes and identify effective methods of intervening. This book summarizes the findings of a project that was commissioned to identify effective treatments.

The policy context during the last decade

In the 1990s research commissioned by the Department of Health showed that on the whole, the UK child protection system intervened too late and did not offer parents sufficient support or preventative services (Department of Health 1995). The subsequent *refocusing initiative* of the late 1990s aimed to move local authority social services away from a primary focus on child protection towards a more holistic, family welfare approach in which 'the threshold for acceptance of a *child protection* referral would be raised, and more cases would be dealt with as *children in need* (Children Act 1989) or *child concern*' (Thorpe and Bilson 1998 in Platt 2006, p.6). These changes were formalized in the *Framework for the Assessment of Children in Need and their Families* (Department of Health 2000) and *Working Together* (Department of Health 1999).

Many of the early concerns that serious child protection issues might not be handled adequately outside child protection procedures (Calder and Hackett 2003) were not supported by the evidence. Indeed, not only was there no evidence of unsafe practice (Corby 2003; Platt 2001) but subsequent studies (Cleaver and Walker 2004; Spratt and Callan 2004) found that the new statutory guidance resulted in greater attention to the building of relationships and to participatory and partnership practice that were more favourable to parents. However, the research also suggested that the shift from a child protection to a child welfare orientation had been hampered by continuing professional and organizational concern to manage risk, one of the consequences being that there appeared to have been only marginal moves in the direction of the new policy (Corby 2003). There also appeared still to be a very high threshold for access to services, with child protection being the surest way to receive an intervention (Corby 2003), despite research suggesting that initial assessments could be extended to include a much wider range of cases (Platt 2006). The observation that employing organizations were restricting the ability of social workers to permit their practice to be more directly driven by research and policy was made by Nigel Parton back in 1997 (see Parton 2004), and subsequent research suggested that this was still the case.

Further policy changes, including those following the Victoria Climbié inquiry (Lord Laming 2003) resulted in major changes to the way in which services and professionals worked together to reduce abuse and neglect in the UK. Some of these recommendations were subsequently enshrined in policy including *Every Child Matters* (Department for Education and Skills 2003), the *National Service Framework for Children, Young People and Maternity*

Services (Department of Health and Department for Education and Skills 2004), and the Children Act 2004 which provided the legislative framework to underpin whole system reform.

These changes represented an important shift in government policy from a focus on child protection to family support and improved parenting. They also recognized the need to locate targeted services within universal services, to intervene early, and to work 'in partnership' with parents (Department of Health and Department for Education and Skills 2004). They resulted in extended early years provision, better integration of health, education and social care via children's centres, parenting support embedded at each life stage, and multidisciplinary teams based in universal services such as clusters of schools or early years settings (Department for Education and Skills 2004). *Aiming High for Children: Supporting Families* (HM Government and Department for Education and Skills 2007) highlighted the need for improved responsiveness through better early intervention including the monitoring of risk and identification of need as early as possible, the provision of tailored support, better targeted support and specialist services, and the shift to a model of progressive universalism. The development of a national intensive home visiting programme beginning during pregnancy and continuing throughout the first two years of life has been one of the first expressions of this emphasis on the perinatal period and beyond (Department for Children, Schools and Families 2007). Other changes aimed specifically at better protecting children have included the development of ContactPoint, a database containing basic demographic information about all children in England and details of the professionals working with them, local authorities leading on multi-agency working via children's trusts, the development of statutory Local Safeguarding Children Boards (LSCBs) to replace non-statutory Area Child Protection Committees (ACPCs), and the development of an integrated inspection framework.

Lord Laming's Progress Report (2009) and the subsequent government response (Department for Children, Schools and Families 2009) emphasized the need for further changes in terms of both national and local leadership and accountability, including the appointment of a chief adviser on the safety of children, and the development of a National Safeguarding Delivery Unit focused on better, more consistent practice, monitoring and reporting on progress, and increased public and professional confidence. Lord Laming's Progress Report pointed to the need for better support for frontline practice including the development of a programme of intensive support and coaching for social work team leaders and frontline managers, better identification and dissemination of effective practice, particularly for children living in families where they are at high risk of being abused or neglected, and rapid research reviews focusing on supporting difficult decisions made by frontline staff, in intervening effectively where there are concerns that a child is likely to suffer harm, and more effective oversight and review of cases in the light of changing circumstances (Department for Children, Schools and Families 2009).

Despite these extensive policy and practice developments there has been little specific focus on emotional maltreatment and a need for clarity at both a policy and practice level about the best ways to intervene in cases of emotional maltreatment. This book aims to address this gap in our knowledge.

General approach

Theories of causation about child abuse have to date generally fallen into three groups:

1. Psychological theories, that focus on the personal history and characteristics of adults who abuse children.

2. Social-psychological theories that focus on the dynamics and interaction between abuser, child and immediate environment.

3. Sociological perspectives that emphasize the way in which social and cultural factors create the conditions for child maltreatment.

Each of these models has made an important contribution to our understanding of the factors involved in all types of child abuse.

More recently an ecological-transactional model (see Table 1.1) has been developed, which focuses on both the specific and heterogeneous risk factors associated with the occurrence of abuse. It also acknowledges the dynamic and reciprocal contributions made by the environment, child and parent in terms of a child's development (Cicchetti and Carlson 1995; Cicchetti and Lynch 1993). Within this model 'maltreatment is treated as representing a dysfunction in the parent–child-environment system rather than solely the result of aberrant parental traits or environmental stress or deviant child characteristics' (Cicchetti and Carlson 1995, p381).

Table 1.1 Ecological/transactional model

Temporal dimension	Potentiating factors	Compensatory factors
Enduring factors	Vulnerability factors: Enduring factors/conditions increasing risk of harm	Protective factors: Enduring factors/conditions that decrease risk of harm
Transient factors	Challengers: Transient but significant stressors	Buffers: Transient conditions which buffer stress

The above framework provides the scope to conceptualize the complex causes of maltreatment in terms of both potentiating factors that make the child more vulnerable, and compensatory factors which help to protect the child. It also includes a temporal element, which recognizes that some factors may be transient, while others are more enduring, alongside recognition of the multiple ecological levels within which such transactions take place (see Chapter 9 for further discussion).

Preventing the occurrence and recurrence of emotional maltreatment

Maltreatment is an exposure, and not a symptom or disease, and we have therefore used the following framework (See Figure 1.1 below) to identify possible points for intervening. Prevention before it has occurred can involve the use of both universal interventions that are in principle available to everyone (see Chapter 5) and targeted interventions that are directed at children who are at particular risk of being abused or neglected (see Chapter 6). After maltreatment has occurred or been identified, the aim is to prevent its recurrence (i.e. using interventions that target parents with a view to preventing further maltreatment), and to prevent further impairment (i.e. using interventions that target children with a view to preventing further decline in their wellbeing and promoting future health). The focus of this book is the effectiveness of interventions or services that are aimed at preventing the occurrence or recurrence of emotional maltreatment.

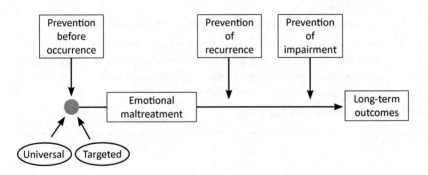

Figure 1.1 Framework for intervention

Methodology

There has to date been limited research on how to treat adults who maltreat children emotionally. The aim of this review was to collate recently published evidence about 'what works' in preventing the *occurrence* and *recurrence* of emotional maltreatment. In order to do this we searched a range of electronic databases to identify published studies that had evaluated the effectiveness of any intervention, treatment or service, directed at the parents of children aged 0–19 years, and aimed at preventing emotional maltreatment (see Appendix 1 for further detail about the search). We did not include evaluations of interventions or services that were directed at the prevention of impairment (i.e. tertiary prevention). The aim was to identify programmes, interventions or services directed at parents alone, parents and children, or families (but not children alone) (see Box 1.1). We further specified that to be included in the review, studies had to have a component that was intended to change or improve parenting, and to have targeted parents defined as emotionally abusive (see Chapter 2 for further discussion). It also had to have evaluated the benefit of the intervention in terms of its impact on parental attitudes or behaviours particularly with regard to the occurrence of emotional maltreatment (including the child ceasing to be the subject of a child protection plan where appropriate). Where available we have also reported data about the impact on children's social, emotional or psychological wellbeing.

Box 1.1 Study inclusion criteria

Included studies had to have:

- evaluated a parent- or parent–child or family-focused intervention
- included a component that was intended to change or improve parenting
- focused primarily on parents defined as emotionally abusive
- included direct assessments of emotional abuse (e.g. children who are the subject of a child protection plan) or proxy measures such as parental functioning (e.g. misattributions or anger) or child outcomes (e.g. abuse or wellbeing)
- been published since 1990.

Appraising the evidence

Critical appraisal is the process by which the methodological rigour of research studies is assessed in order to judge the reliability of the results, and how confident we can be that the findings are sufficiently strong to enable us to base future practice on them.

Each of the included studies has been critically appraised using standard criteria that have been developed to enable researchers to assess the most important aspects of methodology. We have chosen not to rate each study in terms of the total number of criteria that are met, because the individual criteria do not have equal weighting. We have therefore rated each study by allocating it a grade that is based on the overall study design (see Box 1.2). The highest level of evidence is randomized controlled trials (RCTs) and has been indicated by the letter A; the second highest level of evidence (e.g. non-randomized studies that have utilized a control or comparison group) has been allocated the letter B; the third highest level of evidence (e.g. studies with an intervention group only that collected data pre- and post-intervention) has been allocated the letter C; retrospective quantitative studies have been allocated the letter D; and case studies have been allocated the letter E. The recommendations that have been made at the end of each chapter have been adjusted to take account of the results of this appraisal, and we have urged caution where the study has highlighted a new or in-novative way of working, but where the evaluation as to whether it works was not rigorous.

Box 1.2 Evidence levels*

A – Randomized controlled trial
B – Non-randomized controlled study
C – One group pre- and post-intervention
D – Retrospective quantitative studies
E – Case studies

---

*The evaluation of effectiveness in an intervention group by only measuring aspects of child and family functioning before the intervention and after it

Strengths and limitations

This is one of the first reviews of the evidence about 'what works' to prevent the occurrence and recurrence of emotional maltreatment, and we have tried to be as inclusive as possible. We sought to include a wide range of studies, not limiting the search to the current gold standard of randomized control-led trials. This ensured that we identified innovative methods of working, even if these had not been rigorously evaluated.

The primary focus on evidence about the prevention of the *occurrence* and *recurrence* of emotional maltreatment meant that it was not possible to include evidence about 'what works' in terms of preventing impairment. This is a significant omission because children who have experienced emotional maltreatment suffer a range of problems as a result of the impact of the abuse on their development and wider functioning (see Chapter 2). Once emotional maltreatment has been identified, interventions that are aimed at improving the functioning of the child are necessary alongside those that are aimed at preventing further abuse by focusing on parenting and family relationships more generally, and a review of these is now needed.

The content of this book has been circumscribed by what is available in terms of published evaluation studies. The assessment and treatment of emotional maltreatment is in its early days, and there are still very few published evaluations on this topic. The available evidence is also mixed in terms of the rigour with which included studies have been conducted and of the types of emotional maltreatment that have been targeted. One of the issues that will be addressed in each of the findings chapters and in the final section on the implications for policy and practice, is the extent to which the type of emotionally abusive parenting that has been targeted by the studies that we identified, is representative of the type of emotionally abusive parenting that practitioners are likely to encounter in everyday practice.

Organization of the book

The book has been organized into four sections. The first section examines a range of background issues that are relevant to an understanding about what is meant by emotional maltreatment;[1] section two presents the findings about 'what works' in preventing the *occurrence* of maltreatment; section three presents the findings about what works in preventing the *recurrence* of emotional maltreatment; and section four examines in more detail the implications of the results for practitioners and the provision of services more generally.

Section One – Emotional Maltreatment and its Consequences

Chapter 2 examines what we mean by 'emotional maltreatment', how common it is, and what are the associated problems. A number of illustrations of different types of emotional maltreatment have been provided.

Section Two – Preventing the Occurrence of Emotional Maltreatment

Chapters 3 and 4 examine the evidence about the effectiveness of population-based and targeted interventions respectively that are aimed at preventing the *occurrence* of emotional maltreatment. These chapters examine the

---

1   We have used the term maltreatment throughout to refer to emotional abuse and neglect. The term emotional abuse is sometimes used by other authors, but does not necessarily include emotional neglect.

defining characteristics of the two types of preventive methods alongside the type of factors that might be targeted and evidence about the effectiveness of such methods of working.

Section Three – Preventing the Recurrence of Emotional Maltreatment

Chapters 5, 6 and 7 examine the findings of studies about three types of intervention – parent-focused; parent/child-focused; and family-focused, respectively. Each of the chapters has a similar format and explores the aetiological and theoretical models underpinning the interventions being evaluated in the included studies; the findings of individual studies in terms of the intervention and populations targeted and the outcomes; and the strengths and limitations of the evidence.

Section Four – Implications for Practice

Chapter 8 examines the key findings from sections two and three in the light of what is known about the treatment of abuse more generally, and Chapter 9 examines the implications of the findings for policy makers, service commissioners and practitioners in terms of what needs to be done to apply the evidence to everyday practice. We have concluded with a number of recommendations that have emerged from the findings of the review, and that we feel would improve practice in relation to the identification and management of emotional maltreatment.

2

What is Emotional Maltreatment?

Introduction

Emotional maltreatment, sometimes referred to as psychological maltreatment (see below for further discussion), has only recently been recognized as a problem in its own right. This may be due in part to the fact that it is an aspect of all types of abuse. However, it also occurs alone and when it does, it tends to elude detection and intervention (Behl, Conyngham and May 2003; Glaser, Prior and Lynch 2001; Ward *et al.* 2004).

It is the type of emotional maltreatment that occurs on its own that is the focus of this book, and this chapter examines what is meant by the term 'emotional maltreatment', and how common it is now thought to be. It describes some of the consequences associated with it, and explores some of the issues related to its detection and the prevention of its recurrence.

What is emotional maltreatment?

The lack of a universally agreed definition has made it difficult to identify emotional maltreatment, and it is possibly the most under-reported and least studied form of abuse (Barnett, Miller-Perrin and Perrin 2005). Difficulties in defining emotional maltreatment may reflect the fact that it comprises a 'relationship that exists between the parent and child, rather than a specific event or series of events' that can be readily identified (Glaser 2002, p.702). This makes it harder to achieve societal consensus regarding the difference between emotional abuse and suboptimal parenting (Trickett *et al.* 2009). Furthermore, this category of abuse encompasses behaviour that ranges from neglect, lack of responsiveness or lack engagement to behaviour which is consistently intrusive, hostile, critical and controlling (Hart, Binggeli and Brassard 1998). Emotional maltreatment may take the form of acts of commission, such as verbal abuse, spurning, terrorizing, and isolating, or of omission, such as ignoring, being psychologically unresponsive or unavailable (Brassard and Donovan 2006). Not all emotionally abusive parenting involves negative affect, however, and parents' unresolved trauma and loss can be expressed, for example, as fear for and over-protectiveness of a much loved child, resulting in the child's inability to negotiate normal developmental hurdles (Boulton and Hindle 2000).

Typically, child emotional maltreatment involves behaviour of caregivers (verbal or nonverbal, active or passive, and intended or not) that has the potential to damage the social, cognitive, emotional and physical development of a child. Essentially, it refers to a constant, repeated pattern of parental behaviour that is likely to be interpreted by a child that she or he is unloved, unwanted, serves only instrumental purposes, and which severely undermines children's development and socialization (Glaser 2002).

Box 2.1 Description of emotional abuse

Emotional abuse is the sustained, repetitive, inappropriate, emotional responses to the child's felt emotions and their accompanying expressive behaviour. Emotional abuse impedes emotional development. In babies, it also impedes the onset of speech development. It retards the process through which a child acquires the ability to feel and express different emotions appropriately, and eventually, to regulate and control them. It impacts adversely on (a) the child's educational, social and cultural development; (b) psychological development; (c) relationships in adulthood; and (d) career prospects. (O'Hagan 2006, p.46)

Recent publications in the field have distinguished between emotional and psychological abuse, the latter referring explicitly to caregiving that has an adverse impact in terms of the child's mental faculties and processes (e.g. memory, attention, recognition, perception, intelligence, and moral reasoning). O'Hagan, for example, writes with regard to this that 'The attack upon perceptual development is most serious in the sustained long-term sensory deprivations inflicted on babies and infants who are made to spend long hours in their cots or prams, in smoke-filled rooms, starved of natural light and human interaction. Perceptual deprivation is often neither recognized not acknowledged yet it is one of the most common forms of psychological abuse. It has a profound, adverse impact upon the development of other crucially important mental faculties as well as on children's social, educational and psychological development as a whole' (2006, p.56).

Glaser and Prior (2002) have proposed five categories of emotional abuse and neglect (Box 2.2) that integrate the work of theorists and practitioners in Europe, US, UK and elsewhere, and that we believe incorporates the type of caregiving that O'Hagan refers to as psychological abuse. Although in practice these behaviours often overlap, this framework can help practitioners to observe and think about situations that are often discordant and difficult to understand and manage, and to highlight the many ways in which children experience emotional maltreatment (Boulton and Hindle 2000).

Box 2.2 Categories of emotional maltreatment

The five categories comprise:

- emotional unavailability, unresponsiveness and neglect
- negative attributions and misattributions to the child
- developmentally inappropriate or inconsistent interactions with the child
- failure to recognize the child's individuality and emotional boundaries
- failure to promote the child's social adaptation.

(Glaser and Prior 2002)

Emotional unavailability, unresponsiveness and neglect

Emotional unavailability, unresponsiveness and neglect usually occurs when primary carers are so preoccupied with their own difficulties (including mental illness) or practices (such as substance abuse) or external commitments, that they are unable to respond to the child's emotional needs, and make no provision for an alternative.

Negative attributions and misattributions to the child

Negative attributions and misattributions towards a child are one of the most common forms of emotional abuse, and possibly one of the most easy to recognize. Negative attributions involve the parent attributing characteristics to a child that are negative and belittling. One of the consequences of negative attributions is that if they are sufficiently protracted, they can be internalized by the child and become an integral part of the child's sense of self (Lieberman 1997). It includes hostility that is focused directly at the child or at the child via another person. It also includes denigration and rejection of the child. A parent may also be emotionally unresponsive if the child is percieved as not deserving affection and attention.

Developmentally inappropriate or inconsistent interactions with the child

Developmentally inappropriate or inconsistent interactions with the child include the parent having expectations of the child beyond his or her developmental capabilities, and may include role reversal in which 'parentification' occurs (i.e. whereby the child takes on the role of the parent). It may also include over-protection, the limitation of exploration and learning, and exposure to confusing or traumatic events and interactions. The latter may include witnessing violence towards a loved one, parental para-suicide and solvent abuse.

Failure to recognize the child's individuality and emotional boundaries

Failure to recognize the child's individuality and emotional boundaries can involve using the child for the fulfilment of the parent's emotional needs and inability to distinguish between the child's reality and the adult's beliefs and wishes.

Failure to promote the child's social adaptation

Failure to promote the child's social adaptation can include forms of mis-socialization such as exposing a child to corrupt, illegal or violent activities including substance misuse and failing to provide for a child's developmental needs for education, cognitive development and experiential learning. This category also includes the isolation of children.

Based on a recent overview of the literature, Brassard and Donovan (2006) developed six categories of abusive parent/caregiver behaviour (in contrast to categories that are based on maladaptive development of the child), each containing a further two to five subcategories (Table 2.1).

..1 Six categories of emotional abuse

..ing	Belittling, denigrating or other rejecting Ridiculing for showing normal emotions Singling out; humiliating in public
Terrorizing	Placing in unpredictable/chaotic circumstances Placing in recognizably dangerous situations Having rigid/unrealistic expectations accompanied by threats if not met; threatening/perpetrating violence against child Threatening/perpetrating violence against child's loved ones/objects – includes exposure to intimate partner violence (IPV)
Isolating	Confining within environment Restricting social interactions in community
Exploiting/corrupting	Modelling, permitting or encouraging antisocial behaviour Modelling, permitting or encouraging developmentally inappropriate behaviour Restricting/undermining psychological autonomy Restricting/interfering with cognitive development
Denying emotional responsiveness	Providing little or no warmth, nurturing, praise during any developmental period in childhood
Mental heath/legal/medical neglect	Limiting a child's access to necessary health care due to reasons other than inadequate resources

Source: Brassard and Donovan 2006

Prevalence of emotional maltreatment

Estimates of the extent of emotional maltreatment are influenced by the definition of maltreatment used, and the source of the data. The most conservative estimates are usually produced by official sources of data such as the number of children who are the subject of a child protection plan. This under-represents the extent of the problem because child protection plans are not a measure of the incidence of emotional abuse and because the majority of children who are abused are not referred to child protection services; and those who become the subject of a child protection plan represent an even smaller proportion of the total (Evans 2002). In the UK, data from government statistics shows that emotional abuse is now the second most common form of maltreatment. Table 2.2 shows the percentage of children who have been the subject of a child protection plan in England by category of abuse.

Table 2.2 Percentage of Children subject of a child protection plan in England by category of abuse 2004–2008

	2004	2005	2006	2007	2008
Neglect	41	43	43	44	45
Physical abuse	19	18	16	15	15
Sexual abuse	9	9	8	7	7
Emotional abuse	18	19	21	23	25
Multiple	14	12	11	10	8

Source: DCSF 2008

The most up-to-date estimates of the reasons for children being the subject of a child protection plan for emotional abuse showed that 'the commonest form of ill-treatment was "developmentally inappropriate interaction with the child", which was experienced by 42 per cent of the children; denigration or rejection affected 34 per cent of the children, followed by emotional unavailability, unresponsiveness or neglect (28%)' (Glaser *et al.* 2001 in Evans 2002, pp.iii–iv). Other research showed that these children 'most frequently experienced fear-inducing caregiver abusive behaviour (95% of children affected)' and that 'other categories of caregiver abusive behaviour experienced by these children were as follows: inappropriate roles (92%); rejection (86%); isolating (54%); degrading (53%); ignoring (28%); corrupting (19%); tormenting (18%)' (Doyle 1997, p.336).

Evidence from self-reports, however, suggests a much higher prevalence than is indicated by the number of children who are the subject of a child protection plan. A recent systematic review of the burden and consequences of emotional abuse, for example, concluded that results from large population-based, self-report studies in the UK and US showed that approximately 8–9 per cent of women and about 4 per cent of men reported exposure to severe emotional abuse during childhood (Gilbert *et al.* 2009). The rates in adults are similar to those recorded in the past year in boys and girls (10.3%), and even higher rates have been reported in Eastern European countries using similar measures (Box 2.3) (Gilbert *et al.* 2009).

Box 2.3 Prevalence of emotional abuse

- 10.3% is the yearly prevalence of emotional abuse (verbal abuse by adults or told not wanted; US study).

- 4–9% is the cumulative prevalence based on categories consistent with severe emotional abuse (studies in Sweden, USA and UK).

- 12.5–33.3% is the yearly prevalence of severe or moderate emotional abuse reported for four Eastern European states (Macedonia, Latvia, Lithuania and Moldova).

The most recent estimate in the UK was obtained from a national survey of 2869 18–24-year-olds, which found that six per cent reported frequent and severe emotional control and domination, psycho/physical control and domination, humiliation, attacks on self-esteem, withdrawal of their primary carer's attention/affection, antipathy, terrorizing or threatening behaviours and proxy attacks. Around one-third of the sample had experienced 'terrorizing' including threats to harm the child or someone or something the child loves, threatening with fear figures, and threats to have the child sent away (Cawson *et al.* 2000).

These data strongly suggest that emotional maltreatment is common and that a central part of its management should involve the use of preventive interventions aimed at helping high-risk and vulnerable parents to develop healthier ways of relating to children, in addition to the use of child protection procedures.

Factors associated with emotional abuse

Although emotional abuse occurs in a wide range of families, it is also associated with multiple stresses (Doyle 1997 in Evans 2002, p.335), and in particular with factors such as domestic violence, adult mental health problems, and parental substance misuse (Department of Health 1999). For example, one study showed that '28 per cent of mothers and 23 per cent of father figures of registered children were referred for help with drink problems, and domestic violence was a central issue in 26 per cent of register cases and a peripheral one in 28 per cent' (Doyle 1997 in Evans 2002, p.335).

The following four sections examine some of the factors associated with emotional maltreatment in more detail.

Mental health problems

In the US two-thirds of adults who meet the criteria for psychiatric disorders across all diagnostic conditions are parents (Hinden 2006, p.21). However, there is currently little attention paid to the effect of mental illness on their ability to meet the emotional needs of their children. Recent research suggested that frontline practitioners perceive parenting to be adversely affected in a significant majority (around half) of parents with mental health problems (Dent and McIntyre 2000). It is also recognized, however, that its consequences for the child may be mediated by a range of factors such as household financial stress, partner conflict, the social and family support systems available, and individual children's coping skills (Doyle 1997). For example, an early study of the resilient children of psychotic parents drew attention to the mediating, protective role of parental warmth (Kauffman *et al.* 1979).

Some parental mental health problems are, however, associated with unpredictable and frightening behaviours, while others (particularly depression) are linked with parental withdrawal and neglect (Loh and Vostanis 2004; Foster, Garber and Durlak 2008). The adverse effects of maternal caregiver depression on the wellbeing of children, and in particular the under-fives, is well documented (Beardslee *et al.* 1983), and a meta-analysis found that depression was associated with negative maternal behaviour and was also evident to a somewhat lesser degree in terms of the mother's disengagement from the child (Lovejoy *et al.* 2000). This finding was confirmed by a number of more recent studies, which showed that maternal depression was related to lower levels of maternal sensitivity (Trapolini, Ungerer and McMahon 2008), less empathic understanding of toddlers (Coyne *et al.* 2007), higher intrusiveness, negative regard and harsh behaviour, lower warmth, more negative perceptions of infant behaviour and greater hostility towards infants (Kolozian 2007), rejection of the infant and maternal pathological anger (Loh and Vostanis 2004), and less contingent/affective attunement to infant behaviour (Stanley, Murray and Stein 2004). The evidence also shows that maternal depression is associated with fewer positive and more negative behaviours towards older (i.e. adolescent) children (Foster *et al.* 2008). The timing and severity of maternal depression is important, since it appears most harmful to children when it affects the first five years of life (Zahn-Waxler, Duggal and Gruber 2002).

Anxiety disorders, including panic disorder and phobias, are one of the most widespread mental health problems (Turner *et al.* 2003). Although there has been little research on the effects of anxiety on parenting, parents who suffer from severe anxiety have been observed to be highly critical, express less affection, smile less, be more likely to over-react during interactions with their children, and appear to be less likely to encourage emotional autonomy, for example, by soliciting their child's opinion or tolerating differences of opinion (Turner *et al.* 2003, p.542).

Psychotic disorders that involve distortions of thought, perception and communication, and significant restrictions in the range and intensity of emotional expression, are associated with greater difficulties in fulfilment of daily parenting roles, less positive affect, less responsiveness to children, more limited environmental stability and lower levels of sensory and motor stimulation (Zahn-Waxler *et al.* 2002). Schizophrenia can cause significant impairment to parenting. One recent study found that compared with a diagnosis of psychotic depression, schizophrenia was highly significantly associated with social services supervision and staff-rated problems with emotional responsiveness, practical baby care, and perceived risk of harm to the baby (Zahn-Waxler *et al.* 2002). A further study showed that mothers with schizophrenia had greater 'interactive deficits' and were more remote, insensitive, intrusive and self-absorbed (Wan *et al.* 2007, p.537), there being some evidence that the relationship between maternal mental illness and compromised mother–infant interaction may be partially mediated by levels of cognitive function (Steadman *et al.* 2007).

Practitioners, however, are perhaps understandably reluctant to describe the often erratic, inconsistent and even frightening behaviours that can result as a consequence of severe mental illness as emotional maltreatment, and there is currently very little attention paid to the needs of children whose parents have severe mental illness.

Substance abuse

In the US, around 80 per cent of women who abuse drugs are of childbearing age (National Centre on Addiction and Substance Abuse 1996) and have multiple, compounded psychopathology, and histories of abuse and neglect. Luthar and Suchman (2000) whose work has focused on drug-abusing mothers and Luthar, Suchman and Altomare (2007), have postulated that the factors that put women at risk of drug abuse (such as childhood abuse and poor social supports) also increase the risk of child maltreatment. However, they have also observed that contrary to what is sometimes assumed, substance-abusing women often desire to be good mothers and can be aware of what good parenting involves, but feel unable to fulfil this role (see also Roldan, Galera and O'Brien 2005).

While there is some recognition that parental substance abuse on the part of one or both parents is associated with high rates of child maltreatment (Chaffin, Kelleher and Hollenberg 1996), there is little research addressing the relationship between parental substance abuse and emotional maltreatment more specifically (Straussner and Fewell 2006). The adverse parenting outcomes associated with substance misuse appear to be linked to the multiple difficulties experienced by such parents (e.g. drug use, mental health problems, family relationships, socioeconomic factors, etc.), rather than the drug use *per se* (Dawe and Harnett 2007).

Domestic violence

Domestic violence is more common than previously recognized and a study published in 1995 showed that 45 per cent of a UK sample of adults across the social and age spectrum had witnessed domestic violence at least once, and that 10 per cent had seen it 'constantly' or 'frequently' (Creighton and Russell 1995). Over three decades of research on children who witness domestic violence has shown that it is one of the most serious factors undermining children's cognitive, emotional and even physical wellbeing (Koenen *et al.* 2003; Volpe 1996). Attacks on a parent almost always frighten children even if the child is not the direct target, although a parent (most frequently, but not invariably, the male partner) will sometimes exploit a mother's or child's fears for each other and use threats or actual violence as part of a pattern of aggression (Bifulco and Moran 1998).

It is now recognized that children who witness domestic violence are at a disproportionate risk of injury, eating disorders and self-harm (World Health Organization 2002), even when they are not themselves victims of physical violence. The profound distress caused by this under-studied form of child abuse is associated with girls' increased risk of eating disorders, self-mutilation and of becoming victims of domestic violence in later life (Felitti *et al.* 1998), and of exposure to social violence and permanent impairment to cognitive and sensory growth in both girls and boys (Koenen *et al.* 2003; Wolfe *et al.* 2003).

Despite common misperceptions, domestic violence also has a significant impact on the wellbeing of babies, with one study showing that infants exposed to domestic violence displayed poor health, poor sleeping habits, excessive screaming and attachment disorders (Jaffe, Wolfe and Wilson 1990).

Faltering growth

While the above categories all focus on parental behaviours it has also been suggested that parental behaviour may be an inadequate predictor of emotional abuse and that child outcomes should be the focus of interest including, for example, physical syndromes such as psychosocial short stature and failure to thrive (Kavanagh 1982 in Evans 2002). Faltering growth (non-organic failure to thrive) is one example where acts of omission specifically in terms of a child's emotional needs may result in an infant who falls into the bottom 5 per cent or lower on established growth charts (Wooster 1999). Faltering growth is now recognized to be a consequence of feeding that has become fraught with tension for both caregiver and infant, and/or emotional neglect. The potential consequences of faltering growth to infants' long-term physical and cognitive development are well established (Kerr, Black and Krishanakumar 2000; Mackner, Starr and Black 1997). See Iwaniec (1997a) for a full discussion of this issue.

Consequences of emotional abuse

It has been suggested that emotional abuse may be the most damaging compared to other forms of child maltreatment (Iwaniec 1995) and the reason for this is that the perpetrator is almost invariably the person responsible for enabling children to fulfil their developmental tasks (i.e. the primary carer) (Glaser 2002). Emotional maltreatment targets children's developmental needs for safety, love, belonging and esteem. The presence of other loving caregivers and supports can, however, be protective against the effects of such maltreatment by a parent (Binggeli, Hart and Brassard 2001). A child who is singled out for maltreatment by several family members faces higher risks than one who has a range of support apart from a rejecting or hostile caregiver, or if the caregiver offers counterbalancing positive behaviour (Binggeli *et al.* 2001).

The impact of emotional maltreatment on children

Precisely because it interferes with a child's developmental trajectory, emotional maltreatment has been linked with disorders of attachment, developmental and educational problems, socialization and difficult behaviour (Iwaniec 1997b; Erickson, Egeland and Pianta 1989). Evidence of significant impairment following emotional maltreatment has been obtained from both retrospective and prospective (i.e. longitudinal) studies.

Retrospective studies

Recent research has confirmed earlier overviews of the evidence that have concluded that emotional maltreatment is associated with a range of long-term deleterious outcomes. For example, one study showed that college students' perceptions of emotional abuse and neglect were significantly linked to later anxiety and depression (Wright, Crawford and Del Castillo 2009). A number of other studies have shown retrospective reports of psychological abuse to be associated with depression and shame (Webb *et al.* 2007), the latter predicting poor psychological functioning, and have also pointed to the effects of verbal violence on a range of outcomes including dissociation, depression, anxiety and anger-hostility (Teicher *et al.* 2006). Other research has shown links between psychological maltreatment in childhood and post-traumatic stress disorder (PTSD) symptomatology (Chirichella-Besemer and Motta 2008), eating disorders in adolescence (Witkiewitz and Dodge-Reyome 2001), dating violence (victimization in females and overall dating violence in males) (Wekerle *et al.* 2009), and adult sexual victimization including assaults involving both force and coercion (Aosved and Long 2005).

Allen (2008) examined the impact of different types of psychological abuse and found that terrorizing was associated with anxiety and somatic concerns, ignoring predicted scores of depression and Borderline Personality Disorder (BPD), and degradation predicted BPD features only. Retrospective studies have also identified specific and unique types of impairment associated with emotional neglect compared with other forms of maltreatment (Schaffer, Yates and Egeland 2009), particularly aggression in later childhood (Kotch *et al.* 2008) and dissociation (this being mediated by schemas of shame and vulnerability to harm) (Wright *et al.* 2009).

The timing, chronicity and severity of emotional maltreatment also appear to mediate its effects on children. For example, more severe general and trauma symptoms and insecure attachment were described in respondents who reported experiencing extreme rejection, extreme threats and extreme isolation (Lopez-Stane 2006).

Prospective studies

While prospective studies about the impairment associated with emotional or psychological maltreatment are much rarer (Schaffer *et al.* 2009), such longitudinal studies are also the most reliable source of evidence about the impact of very *early* emotional maltreatment. However, research during this period focuses primarily on emotional neglect (i.e. in which parents are emotionally and psychologically unavailable, detached, avoidant and unresponsive to a young child's needs). For example, prospective studies have shown emotional unavailability of primary caregivers in early childhood (Erickson *et al.* 1989) and unresponsive and neglectful caregiving (Sturge-Apple, Davies and Cummings 2006) to be associated with a range of later internalizing and externalizing symptoms, including non-compliance, negativistic, impulsive behaviour, high dependence on teachers, nervous signs, self-abusive behaviour and other problems (Egeland, Sroufe and Erickson 1983). Egeland *et al.* (1983) showed a steep decline in the performance of such emotionally neglected toddlers on the Bayley Scales of Infant Development between 9 and 24 months, and found strong associations with anxious attachment by 18 months of age (Egeland *et al.* 1983 in Egeland 2009). By 42 months these children were observed to be 'more angry, noncompliant, lacking in persistence, and displaying little positive affect' (Egeland 2009, p.23). In early school they were 'more socially withdrawn, unpopular with peers, and in general exhibiting more problems of the internalizing type...' (p.23); they were rated as more aggressive and less attentive, and performed less well in terms of grade scores. By adolescence, they exhibited 'higher levels of social problems, delinquency, and aggression', and reported more attempted suicides. The majority received at least one diagnosis of mental illness and 73 per cent were comorbid for two or more disorders (p.23).

In addition to emotional neglect, a number of researchers have examined the impact of actively hostile, *frightening* and *frightened* behaviours by mothers that they called 'atypical' or 'Fr-behaviour' (Main and Hesse 1990), also known as hostile/helpless behaviours (Lyons-Ruth *et al.* 2005). These can be subtle (for example, periods of being dazed and unresponsive) or more overt (deliberately frightening children). Fr-behaviours are distinct from neglect and express a distorted image of the child, which is the consequence of the mothers' unresolved trauma and losses (Jacobvitz *et al.* 1997). Prospective studies have shown that frightened and frightening behaviours of this nature are strongly associated with disorganized attachment in infants (Jacobvitz *et al.* 1997), which in turn appears to be associated with a range of deleterious outcomes including social and cognitive difficulties, and psychopathology (Green and Goldwyn 2002) (see below for further detail).

Social consequences of emotional maltreatment

As well as having profound effects on the individual, emotional maltreatment also carries a significant burden for society, as can be seen in its impact on the care system and the costs of educational failure and crime, and to the health services as a result of poor mental health.

Parent–infant/child relationship

The timing of emotional abuse appears to mediate its effects on children, and its impact can be particularly severe when it occurs during the formative years because the first three years of life are critical to a child's later development. Rapid and extensive growth of the brain and biological systems takes place during this period, and is significantly influenced by the young child's environment, and in particular the early parenting that they receive (Schore 1994). It has been suggested that the profound effect of early emotional maltreatment may be due to the fact that '[w]ithin a developmental perspective, the successful resolution of stage-salient issues increases the probability

---

Box 2.4 Key developmental stages

- **Infancy**: attachment, assistance in regulation of bodily states, emotional regulation).

- **Toddlerhood**: development of symbolic representation and further self-other differentiation, problem-solving, pride, mastery, motivation.

- **Preschool**: development of self-control, use of language to regulate impulses, emotions, store information, predict and make sense of the world, development of verbally mediated or semantic memory, gender identity, development of social relationships beyond immediate family and generalization of expectations about relationships, moral reasoning.

- **Latency age**: peer relationships, adaptation to school environment, moral reasoning.

- **Adolescence**: renegotiation of family roles, identity issues – sexuality, future orientation, peer acceptance, ethnicity, moral reasoning.

- **Young adults**: continued differentiation from family, refinement and integration of identity with particular focus on occupational choice and intimate partners, moral reasoning.

---

of competent functioning in the next developmental period' (Egeland 2009, p.23). For example, success in completing later developmental tasks in latency and adolescence are dependent on the success with which the child meets the earlier tasks of infancy and toddlerhood.

A number of key developmental periods have been identified (Box 2.4) (APSAC 1995, p.26) and each is associated with a developmental task. For example, one of an infant's primary developmental tasks is to form a secure attachment with an adult caregiver, learning in the process to trust others to provide a stable environment and believe in his or her own ability to solicit that care. A caregiver who predominantly rejects a toddler's bid for attention will have a negative effect on the child's sense of self-worth and belief in the availability of others (Binggeli *et al.* 2001).

Early derailment influences all the later developmental tasks that have yet to be achieved, and parenting plays a key role in influencing this trajectory. For example, it is a parent's capacity to foster both a 'safe haven' in response to a child's bids for comforts and a 'secure base' in response to a child's bids to explore, that enable a child to begin to develop a sense of security and trust in the people around them (Berlin 2005). Babies who

Box 2.5 Key aspects of early parenting

- **Sensitivity/attunement**: the use of eye contact, voice-tone, pitch and rhythm, facial expression and touch to convey synchronicity with the infant.

- **Mind-mindedness/reflective function/mentalization**: refer to a parent's capacity to experience their baby as an 'intentional being' with their own personality traits, strengths and sensitivities, rather than just in terms of their physical characteristics and behaviour.

- **Marked mirroring**: happens when a parent shows a contingent response to an infant such as looking sad when the baby is crying. The mirroring is marked, in that it is sufficiently different from the infant's expression to indicate separateness, and thereby that things can be made better.

- **Containment**: this occurs when a parent uses touch, gesture and speech to take on board the infant's powerful feelings and make them more manageable.

- **Reciprocity**: this involves turn-taking and occurs when an infant and adult are *jointly* involved in initiating, sustaining and terminating interactions.

- **Continuity of care**: provides infants with sufficiently continuous caretaking from a small number of key carers to enable them to become securely attached.

experience emotional maltreatment during their formative years are significantly more likely to be 'insecurely' attached, or to have a disorganized/disoriented attachment style (see below for further discussion).

A number of aspects of early parenting (Box 2.5) (see Barlow and Underdown 2008 for an overview) have been identified as being particularly important during this period in establishing a secure foundation for later learning, behaviour and health throughout a child's life, and parents differ in their ability to provide these.

The importance of parental sensitivity has been highlighted by attachment research, which provides 'a conceptual framework and empirical evidence to support the view that quality of parents' responses to their infants' cues and signals is a critical factor in the development of a strong parent–child relationship (or feelings of security in the child)' (Benoit *et al.* 2001, p.614). Parental sensitivity has been shown to be strongly associated with infant attachment security (i.e. parenting that is too *intrusive* or too *passive* being particularly detrimental to the development of attachment security), although it is recognized that parenting behaviours explain only some of the association between parental representations and child attachment (Berlin 2005), this phenomenon being known as the 'transmission gap'.

But what does emotional maltreatment during early infancy comprise? Research has indicated that infants can tolerate some insensitive parenting and still be securely attached, providing that certain other conditions are met (Cassidy *et al.* 2005). These require that 'certain negative behaviors must not be present including frightening behaviour, extremely cold and hostile behaviour, or consistent interference with the infant's attempts to self-soothe' (Cassidy *et al.* 2005, p.41). This has been confirmed by research on 'disorganized/disoriented' attachment patterns in young children in which there is a 'lack of an organized strategy for using a caregiver in times of distress, revealed through odd behaviors (e.g. repeated incomplete approaches to the parents, stilling, failing to seek contact when very distressed) that appear to reflect fear and confusion on the part of the infant' (Benoit *et al.* 2001, p.614). This pattern of attachment is thought to occur 'when the figure who would normally be a source of security is also a source of fear' (Main and Hesse 1992 in Benoit *et al.* 2001, p.615), and is strongly associated with a range of adverse developmental outcomes including social and cognitive difficulties, and a number of aspects of severe psychopathology (Green and Goldwyn 2002).

The prevalence of disorganized/disoriented attachment is high in samples in which there has been known maltreatment or in which the child has been cared for by a parent with a psychiatric diagnosis, but it is also present in community samples (van IJzendoorn, Schuengel and Bakermans Kranenburg 1999 in Benoit *et al.* 2001) and is thought to be associated with unresolved attachment losses in the parent or traumas such as physical and sexual abuse (Main and Hesse 1990). More recent research has identified a range of atypical Fr-behaviours that are strongly associated with disorganized/disoriented attachment including affective communication errors, role/boundary confusion, fearful/disoriented behaviour, instrusiveness/negativity, and withdrawal (Main and Hesse 1990).

Detection and treatment of emotional maltreatment

In spite of the dangers it poses, emotional maltreatment eludes detection and intervention (Behl *et al.* 2003; Glaser *et al.* 2001; Ward *et al.* 2004). Boulton and Hindle (2000) observed:

> We had become increasingly aware that children who were being emotionally abused were often the most vulnerable, but least likely to attract the attention of the child protection system, with

workers feeling impotent in the face of problems which [unlike sexual abuse, physical violence or physical neglect] were difficult to tabulate. (Boulton and Hindle 2000, p.440)

There has also been some debate about the appropriateness of formal child protection processes for dealing with emotional abuse with some suggestion that because emotional abuse consists of a sustained, negative relationship it is incongruent with the child protection system's focus on incidents (Glaser and Prior 1997 in Evans 2002).

The assessment and treatment of emotional abuse has been the subject of recent criticism, and it has been noted that 'the assessment of families of children referred because of concerns about emotional abuse and neglect tended to be low key and to concentrate on "risks", rather than on the needs of the children' (Wilding and Thoburn 1997 cited in Evans 2002, p.6). This research also found that 'cases involving suspected emotional maltreatment were more likely to be subject to section 47 enquiries (44%), with a general assessment of need the next most likely course of action (24%). In 8 per cent of cases there was an assessment for a specific service, and only 3 per cent were immediately provided with a service' (p.6). It is concluded that 'actual or likely emotional harm [to the child] did not appear to be given the priority which earlier research suggests is essential if long-term damage to children's life chances is to be avoided' (p.6).

It has also been suggested that problems of detection and treatment are compounded in the UK by child protection services' tendency to assess children for risk, rather than strengthen the capacity of families to care for children (Wilding and Thoburn 1997), and by an understandable concern to avoid false accusation of innocent parents. As a result, 'referrals framed in terms of neglectful behaviour or emotional abuse are likely at a very early stage to be steered away, not only from the formal child protection system but also, without an adequate assessment of need, from the provision of services' (Wilding and Thoburn 1997 cited in Evans 2002, p.6). Poorer families are also likely to be under greater surveillance than middle class or wealthy ones, in which problems may become evident only as a result of children's externalizing behaviour (Barudy 1998).

A second problem in the UK and elsewhere has been the lack of collaboration, and sometimes actual conflict, between adult mental health and child protection services (Darlington, Feeney and Rixon 2005; Boulton and Hindle 2000). There is a gap between awareness of the risk posed by emotional maltreatment and the importance given to treating the parental behaviour that gave rise to it. However, there is some evidence that early recognition and intervention can influence such interaction and improve outcomes for children (Macdonald 2001). Successful interventions need, however, to be underpinned by a sound theoretical framework and to have clear goals. One of the current difficulties is that little is known about what types of intervention are effective.

Summary

The definition of emotional maltreatment that has been adopted for the purpose of this review was intentionally wide, reflecting both the broader understanding of maltreatment that has now been developed, while also bearing in mind the primary aim of the review. This was to identify evidence-based ways of working to prevent the occurrence and recurrence of emotional maltreatment. This definition is consistent with broader policy developments taking place within the UK and more widely. It is also consistent with broader definitions of abuse, such as that developed by the World Health Organization (2002), which includes not only acts towards the child that have a high probability of causing harm to their health or to any aspect of their development (physical, emotional or social, etc.), but also the failure to provide a developmentally appropriate and supportive environment in which the child can develop the full range of emotional and social competencies commensurate with her or his personal potential.

Recent evidence suggests that the prevalence of emotional maltreatment is high in many developed countries including the UK, and that it occurs in a wide range of families, particularly those experiencing multiple stresses including mental health problems, domestic violence and drug and alcohol abuse. Its consequences are far-reaching due in part to the fact that it undermines the healthy emotional development of children.

The detection of emotional abuse is undermined by difficulties in 'assessing and proving that child development, behaviour and wellbeing have been adversely affected to the point of "significant harm" by the caregiver's emotional maltreatment of the child' (Iwaniec 1997, pp.6–7). Intervening once it has been identified is hampered by a lack of understanding about 'what works' and the current review aims to address this knowledge gap.

Section Two

Preventing the Occurrence of Emotional Maltreatment

3

Population-Based Approaches

Introduction

This chapter examines the findings of our search to identify interventions that can be used to prevent emotional maltreatment before it occurs (see Figure 3.1 below). Primary preventive interventions can be provided universally (i.e. to everyone in the population with the aim of promoting emotionally sensitive parenting) or on a targeted basis to parents who have been defined as being at high risk of emotional maltreatment (i.e. to parents living in areas of socioeconomic disadvantage, teenage parents, etc.). The focus of this chapter is on population-based or universal approaches to the prevention of maltreatment.

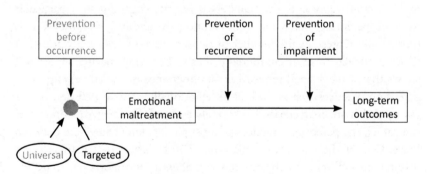

Figure 3.1 Framework for intervention

Population-based or universal interventions

Population-based or universal approaches by definition are aimed at the whole population as opposed to just sections of it. They involve the following:

- An emphasis on the causes of problems at the level of populations rather than the individual.
- Recognition of the need to focus attention on changing behaviour universally.
- A shift of emphasis towards prevention and promotion.

There are a number of important reasons why it makes sense to adopt such an approach. First, evidence from a number of population-based surveys shows that the prevalence of both moderate and severe emotional maltreatment is high. For example, the largest UK population-based survey showed that 6 per cent had experienced serious emotional abuse, and that as many as 30 per cent of the sample had experienced some form of emotional maltreatment (Cawson *et al.* 2000). This is important because it has been recognized that a large number of individuals who are at small risk can give rise to more health problems than a small number of people who are at high risk (Rose 2001), and suggests the need for an approach that can benefit children in the wider population.

Second, most activities, behaviours and problems (including parenting behaviours) have what is known statistically as a 'normal distribution'. This means that if we were to plot emotionally abusive parenting practices on a graph, it would look like Figure 3.2. The vertical Y axis (left-hand side of the graph) represents the number of parents engaging in a particular form of parenting behaviour (i.e. emotionally abusive) and the X axis (horizontal) represents the number of times or severity over a given period that a particular form of emotionally abusive behaviour occurs. Figure 3.2 shows that while a small proportion (at either ends of the curve) engage in parenting practices that are not at all emotionally abusive (left end of the curve) or that are characterized as severely emotionally abusive (right end of the curve), the parenting practices of most parents fall somewhere between these. One of the features of this type of distribution is that there is no 'natural' cut-off between abusive and non-abusive, and *society* has to decide where the threshold should be, with many factors influencing the decisions that practitioners have to make on an individual basis. This means that many children experience abusive parenting practices that are not defined as being sufficiently severe to justify child protection or family support services, but that are nevertheless sufficiently severe to have a significant impact on their development and thereby their life chances.

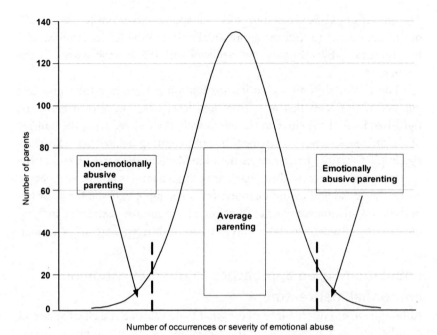

Figure 3.2 Distribution of emotionally abusive parenting practices

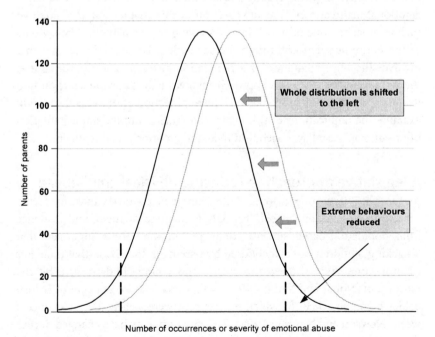

Figure 3.3 Population/universal approach

The aim of population-based or universal approaches is not to use cut-offs of this nature, but to shift the entire distribution to the left as demonstrated by Figure 3.3, by changing the behaviour of the average parent in the population.

The aim of shifting the entire distribution is to reduce the significant number of problems that arise from low level risk, but also to move the right-hand tail of the curve to the left as well, thereby reducing the number of children experiencing extreme forms of parenting behaviours. This strategy implies that the behaviour of the individuals at the extreme end of the spectrum occurs because the behaviour of large numbers of 'average' people create the social and cultural context for other more extreme forms of behaviour. Population approaches therefore aim to improve extreme parenting practices by altering societal norms in terms of different sorts of behaviour.

Population-based approaches to the prevention of emotional maltreatment

Although we did not identify studies that had evaluated the effectiveness of population-based approaches to the prevention of emotional maltreatment, we identified a number of evaluations of the application of such an approach in the reduction of physical child abuse, which may be instructive in terms of emotional maltreatment. The next section of this chapter will examine two such approaches, one of which involves changing the parenting behaviours of the entire population through the use of legislation, and a second that involves the implementation of a population-based parenting programme. We will examine what each approach involves and the evidence regarding its impact on physical child abuse. In the final section of this chapter we will examine the implications of this evidence in relation to the implementation of population-based approaches in reducing emotional maltreatment.

A legislative approach to reducing physical child abuse

At the time of writing a total of 23 European countries have made the 'smacking' of children illegal. The UK is not one of them, and evidence from population-based surveys conducted in the 1990s suggested that 'smacking' children was widely used by parents in the UK at that time. For example, one study showed that babies and young children were hit the most often (Nobes and Smith 1995), with as many as 90 per cent of British babies being smacked, of which 52 per cent were smacked at least once a week (Newson and Newson 1990). This situation may have changed during the last ten years, but we cannot know because there have been no recent estimates of the use of physical punishment in a UK population sample.

Sweden was one of the first countries to make illegal the use of mild forms of corporal punishment including smacking. A national campaign to change parent behaviour was undertaken including the distribution of a 16-page public education brochure, and the printing of information about the change in law on milk cartons for two months (Durrant 1999). Recent evaluation of the impact of this change in law is *suggestive* that the combined use of a legal ban on physical discipline and a health promotion campaign to inform the public about child development was successful in altering both attitudes and behaviour. It found that public support for such punishment had declined from 53 per cent to 11 per cent, and that by 1994 as few as one-third of middle school pupils reported being hit by a parent, and that most had experienced only its mildest forms – 3 per cent harsh slaps and only 1 per cent hit with an object. It also found that individuals raised since the ban were less likely to be suspected of child assault, and for a period of 15 years no child died as a result of abuse in Sweden, and the death rate continues to remain low (Durrant 1999).

It is difficult to be completely confident about attributing these changes solely to the implementation of legislative reform. However, it seems likely that such reform will have played some part in the change that has been witnessed both in the attitudes and behaviours of 'average' parents in the population, and to the more extreme forms of parenting behaviours that are the concerns of child protection agencies.

Other factors that may be contributing to the lower rate of child abuse in Sweden is the holistic approach that is taken towards child protection with the provision of services to all families experiencing problems (Gilbert *et al.* 2009) (see Chapter 9 for further discussion). The next section examines the implementation of a parenting programme using a population-based approach.

A population-based parenting programme

The Triple P-Positive Parenting Programme is 'a multi-level, parenting and family support strategy that aims to prevent severe behavioural, emotional and developmental problems in children by enhancing the knowledge, skills and confidence of parents' (Sanders 1999, p.72). Triple P incorporates five levels of intervention of increasing strength for parents of children from birth to age 12:

- Level 1 – a universal parent information strategy that provides parents with access to information about parenting through a coordinated media and promotional campaign using print and electronic media. This level of intervention aims to increase community awareness of parenting resources, to encourage parents to participate in programmes, and to create a sense of optimism by depicting solutions to common behavioural and developmental concerns.

- Level 2 – a brief, 1- or 2-session primary health care intervention providing anticipatory developmental guidance to parents of children with mild behaviour difficulties, with the aid of user-friendly parenting tip sheets and videotapes that demonstrate specific parenting strategies.

- Level 3 – a 4-session primary care intervention that targets children with mild to moderate behaviour difficulties and includes active skills training for parents.

- Level 4 – an intensive 8- to 10-session individual, group or self-help parenting programme for parents of children with more severe behaviour difficulties.

- Level 5 – an enhanced behavioural family intervention programme for families where parenting difficulties are complicated by other sources of family distress (e.g. relationship conflict, parental depression or high levels of stress).

(Sanders 1999, p.72)

Evidence from rigorous evaluations has shown that parenting programmes provided as part of a public health/population-based approach are effective in improving a number of outcomes (e.g. parenting practices; stress; conflict, etc.) that are significant risk factors for child maltreatment (e.g. Sanders 2008), and recent evidence from the US suggests that the use of this programme was associated with a significant reduction in aggregate measures (including reports and substantiated cases) of child maltreatment (Prinz *et al.* 2009). The US Triple P System Population Trial (Prinz *et al.* 2009) evaluated the effectiveness of disseminating the Triple P-Positive Parenting Programme professional training to the child care workforce across 18 counties, alongside the use of universal media and communication strategies. This strategy resulted in significant proportions of the child care workforce being trained in the delivery of a parenting programme aimed at improving some of the key risk factors for physical child abuse including child emotional and behavioural problems, and parenting stress. An evaluation of this strategy found that compared with the 18 control counties, the intervention counties experienced large statistically and clinically significant reductions in three independently derived population-based predictors of child abuse – substantiated child maltreatment; out of home placements; and child maltreatment injuries (Prinz *et al.* 2009) (see Chapter 8 for further detail). These findings demonstrate the potential value of population-based strategies that are aimed at changing parenting practices on a universal basis (see Figure 3.3).

Population-based approaches to reducing emotional maltreatment

A number of recent UK government policy documents have placed an increased emphasis on the use of preventive and population-based approaches to child protection. These include *Every Child Matters* (Department for Education and Skills 2003), *Aiming High for Children: Supporting Families* (Department for Education and Skills 2007), and the recently revised *Healthy Child Programme* (HCP) (Department of Health 2009), which is part of the *National Service Framework for Children, Young People and Maternity Services* (Department of Health and Department for Education and Skills 2004) and comprises a nationally implemented health promotion and surveillance programme. The HCP incorporates a range of universal strategies that can be used by primary care professionals to promote the type of parenting that is recognized to be important to the emotional wellbeing of young children. This includes, for example, the recommendation that all *routine* contact between professionals and parents be used as an opportunity to promote sensitive and attuned parenting using a range of evidence-based approaches (including media-based strategies such as leaflets; books and videos; skin-to-skin care; use of infant carriers and infant massage, etc.), and to observe and identify parent–infant interaction that requires further input using targeted approaches (Barlow and Svanberg 2009).

While it is unknown whether these strategies lead to the prevention of emotional maltreatment, the above evidence in relation to the use of population-based strategies to reduce physical child abuse suggests that such an approach could be effective.

Summary

A population-based preventive approach is needed because the emotional maltreatment of children is much more prevalent than has been recognized to date and family risk factors, such as problematic parenting and disciplinary practices, are also common. In addition, the majority of children exposed to emotionally abusive parenting practices do not receive services that are aimed at improving their life circumstances. It has also been suggested that there is a need to reduce the population pool of parents who may contribute to potential and substantiated cases of child maltreatment through the use of de-stigmatizing access points (e.g. mass media, primary health care services, schools and child care centres) (Sanders 2008).

We were not able to identify any evidence explicitly evaluating the effectiveness of population-based approaches in reducing emotional maltreatment, but there is preliminary evidence that such approaches (including legislative changes, and the application of parenting programmes on a universal basis) can play a significant role in reducing physical child abuse. Parenting programmes, for example, have been shown to improve many factors associated with child maltreatment, such as family functioning, parental depression, stress, conflict, efficacy and competence. Recent policy initiatives in the UK involving the application of population-based approaches as part of a model of progressive universalism, could potentially contribute to a reduction in emotionally harmful parenting practices, and thereby to a reduction in emotional maltreatment.

4

Targeted Approaches

Introduction

The focus of the last chapter was on the use of universal/population-based approaches to prevent the *occurrence* of emotional maltreatment. These approaches are by definition aimed at everyone. Targeted approaches (see Figure 4.1), on the other hand, are aimed at particular sectors of the population, and therefore require some clarity in terms of the factors that can be used to identify eligible groups or individuals. This chapter describes the way in which such approaches might be used to prevent emotional maltreatment, alongside the available evidence about their effectiveness.

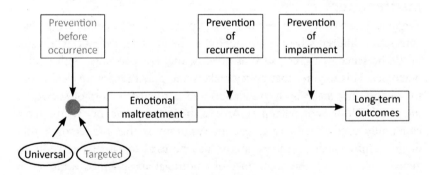

Figure 4.1 Framework for intervention

Targeted approaches to prevention

Targeted approaches to prevention have a number of benefits. First, they enable a more efficient and cost-effective delivery of services by focusing on sectors of the population that require them most. For example, some types of intensive intervention such as home visiting programmes are expensive to deliver and evidence suggests that their long-term cost-effectiveness is dependent on the targeting of the service to socioeconomically deprived, first-time, teenage parents. There is also evidence to suggest that the delivery of interventions of this sort to populations who may not be in need of them can undermine the skills and confidence of parents. For example, one study found slightly worse outcomes for women who received additional post-natal support compared with women who received standard care (Morrell *et al.* 2000).

Targeting also allows the design and delivery of interventions that are aimed at meeting the specific needs of small sectors of the population. For example, Sure Start Local Children's Centres (SSLCs) were focused on supporting the early health and learning needs of groups of disadvantaged children whose development was likely to be compromised as a result of poverty and other associated problems (e.g. parental mental health problems, drug abuse, domestic violence and compromised parenting). One of the key difficulties with such an approach, however, relates to the identification of appropriate criteria with which to target families and the associated stigma of being targeted. These issues are addressed in the next section of this chapter.

Targeted approaches to preventing emotional maltreatment

Targeted interventions or services are typically aimed at improving outcomes for children who are considered to be at increased risk as a result of the presence of factors, such as poverty, that are associated with poorer outcomes. This requires that policy makers and practitioners are clear about the factors that make both individuals and particular sectors of society at increased risk of poor outcomes. As was suggested above, one of the most commonly used criteria to target interventions is that of demographics or geography. Such a strategy might also be used to target interventions aimed at preventing the occurrence of emotional abuse which is higher in socioeconomically deprived families.

Additional criteria that might also be used to identify families at risk of emotional maltreatment include domestic violence, adult mental health problems and parental substance misuse, all of which increase the likelihood of emotional abuse (see Chapter 2).

In addition to these broad indicators, a number of aspects of the early parent–child relationship have been shown to be strongly associated with poor outcomes for children, and the evidence suggests that severe maternal insensitivity (see below for further detail) is an *early* indicator of emotional maltreatment that could be used to target early interventions. The next section examines the use of parenting assessment to target interventions as part of a model of progressive universalism.

Assessing (early) parenting

While many criteria for targeting interventions aimed at preventing emotional maltreatment can be readily identified by practitioners using clinical skills, interviewing techniques and screening tools (e.g. the presence of drug abuse, domestic violence or severe mental health problems), assessing early parenting is more complex. The policy context for such assessment is, however, now in place, and recent policy documents introduced the concept of 'progressive universalism' and highlighted the importance of locating targeted interventions within universal services (Department for Education and Skills 2007). The recently revised *Healthy Child Programme* (Department of Health 2009) indicates that observation of parent–child interaction should be undertaken *routinely* by primary care professionals such as midwives, health visitors and GPs, who have regular contact with parents. A number of methods of *formal* assessment are available to help practitioners to identify early parent–child interactional problems.

Parent–baby and parent–toddler interaction can be formally assessed using methods such as the Alarm Distress Baby Scale (ADBB) (www.adbb.net/gb-intro) or the CARE-Index (www.patcrittenden.com/care-index), in which training is available in the UK. For example, the ADBB can be used to assess social withdrawal behaviour in infants under three years of age and is undertaken by assessing their social responses to the clinician (rather than the parent). Withdrawn social behaviour from just two months old is indicated by 'a lack of either positive (e.g. smiling, eye contact) or negative (e.g. vocal protestations) behaviours' (Guedeney and Fermanian 2001), and should alert practitioners to problems with the infant's environment. The scale involves practitioners assessing eight items, each rated from zero to four (with low scores being optimal social behaviour) including: facial expression; eye contact; general level of activity; self-stimulation gestures; vocalizations; briskness of response to stimulation; relationship to the observer; and attractiveness to the observer. A total ADBB cut-off score of 4–5 has been found to be optimal in detecting infants considered to have unusually low social behaviour.

While this instrument has been validated across a range of populations it has not so far been used to differentiate abusing from non-abusing parents. The CARE-Index (Crittenden 1981), however, has been shown to differentiate abusing from neglecting, abusing-and-neglecting, marginally maltreating and adequate dyads. It enables trained practitioners to observe (ideally using three minutes of videotape of parent–infant/toddler interaction) seven aspects of behaviour assessing affect, cognition and interpersonal contingency. It provides assessments of sensitivity, control and unresponsiveness for the adult; cooperativeness, compulsiveness, difficultness and passivity for the infant (birth to 15 months); and cooperativeness, compulsiveness, threateningly coercive and disarmingly coercive for the toddler (15–30 months) (Crittenden 1981). This assessment provides the practitioner with some indication of the severity of the problems, and the nature of the intervention required. For example, it is suggested that scores of 5–6 (out of 14) indicate the need for parent education; 3–4 indicate the need for parent intervention; and 0–2 points to the need for parent psychotherapy and child protection procedures. Crittenden observes that the need for and nature of the intervention should be based on the use of the CARE-Index *as part of a broader assessment of functioning*, and recent research points to the value of such tools when they are conducted as part of a broader procedure for assessing parents' capacity for change (see below for further discussion).

Tools such as the CARE-Index can be used not only to target or identify parents at risk of emotional maltreatment, but also to focus intervention, because it helps practitioners to identify whether the problem lies with parental affect or cognitions. It also helps them to identify the extent to which the problem is the result of over-intrusiveness or passivity. It is brief and can be used across a range of settings including home, clinic or office, and enables practitioners to identify high-risk dyads, many of which are missed in so-called 'live' assessments (Crittenden 1981), such as, for example, covert parental hostility and infant compulsiveness. The CARE-Index can also be used as an intervention to improve maternal sensitivity (see below for further discussion).

Parent–child interaction involving older children can be assessed using other structured assessment methods including the dyadic Parent–Child Interaction Coding System II (Eyberg *et al.* 1994), which records the frequency of discrete parent and child behaviours, and can distinguish abusive from non-abusive parenting. An alternative is the Emotional Availability Scales (Biringen 2000), which rates several dimensions including parental sensitivity, parental structuring, parental non-intrusiveness, parental non-hostility, child responsiveness and child involvement. As with the CARE-Index, such instruments should be used as part of a broader clinical assessment of functioning, to identify actual emotional abuse or seriously suboptimal parenting in order to target interventions and services more effectively.

What targeted interventions have been evaluated?

The research regarding the relationship between parents' internal working models (also known as parental representations), parental behaviours and child–parent attachment has given rise to a focus on two types of intervention that are of relevance in terms of the targeted prevention of emotionally abusive parenting during the early years (see Chapters 2, 5 and 6 for a more detailed description of these interventions).

Interventions focusing on parental representations

Interventions that are focused primarily on changing parental internal working models include parent–infant and parent–child psychotherapy. While such approaches have on the whole been underpinned by psycho-therapeutic theory, recent research has demonstrated the effectiveness of combined psychotherapeutic (i.e. representational) and behavioural approaches to working with parents and their children, such as for example, Watch, Wait and Wonder (Box 4.1) (Cohen *et al.* 1999, 2000).

Box 4.1 Watch, Wait and Wonder

Watch, Wait and Wonder is a child led psychotherapeutic approach that specifically and directly uses the infant's spontaneous activity in a free play format to enhance maternal sensitivity and responsiveness, the child's sense of self and self-efficacy, emotion regulation, and the child–parent attachment relationship. The approach provides space for the infant/child and parent to work through developmental and relational struggles through play. Also central to the process is engaging the parent to be reflective about the child's inner world of feelings, thoughts and desires, through which the parent recognizes the separate self of the infant and gains an understanding of her own emotional responses to her child. Because of the central role of the infant/child in the intervention and the relationship focus, Watch, Wait and Wonder differs from other interventions which tend to focus primarily on the more verbal partner, the parent. (Cohen *et al.* 2000, available at http://watchwaitandwonder. com)

More recently, the development of relationship-based programmes has been underpinned by research about the importance of 'mentalization' (see Box 2.5.), and of increasing parental 'reflective capacity'. Such interventions include a range of techniques such as, for example, the combined use of family nurse home visiting with infant–parent psychotherapy that is aimed specifically at addressing 'relationship disruptions that stem from mothers' early trauma and derailed attachment history' (Slade *et al.* 2005, p.75) (see Chapter 6 for further detail).

Interventions that are focused on changing parental behaviours

Interventions that are focused on changing parental behaviours are aimed at helping parents to engage in more sensitive interactions with their children and, as such, change to parental representations is regarded as secondary to behavioural change. Interventions of this nature include parent-focused developmental guidance that provides parents with information about their baby's abilities, important developmental milestones and practical caretaking advice. It also includes dyadic interventions such as video-interaction guidance, which involves observation of both parent and infant with a view to providing supportive feedback aimed at helping parents to attend better to infant cues (see, for example, Svanberg 2009), and home visiting programmes such as the Family Nurse Partnership (FNP) (see, for example, Rowe 2009), both of which are being used on a targeted basis in the UK.

Which targeted interventions work?

A recent systematic review of a range of 'attachment-based' interventions, including those referred to above, found 70 studies that had one of four goals:

1. improving maternal sensitivity

2. improving maternal internal working models (e.g. representations)

3. enhancing parental social support

4. a combination of these.

This review found that the most effective interventions focused on improving maternal sensitivity, and that studies showing large effects for sensitivity ($d > 0.40$) also showed large effects for infant attachment ($d = 0.45$) (Berlin 2005).[2] The authors of this review concluded that 'less is more' because they found overall that brief, behaviourally-focused interventions that started six months postnatally were the most effective in improving infant attachment security.

These findings were in contrast with those of an earlier review of such interventions (Egeland *et al.* 2000), which concluded that '*more is better*', and in which the authors recommended more lengthy interventions aimed at

---

2   An effect size (Cohen's *d*) is a way of quantifying the difference between two groups. An effect size of 0.2 indicates no difference between the groups, 0.5 a medium difference, and 0.8 and above a large difference.

improving infant attachment by changing maternal internal working models in addition to parenting behaviours (Berlin 2005). In an attempt to address these diverging conclusions Berlin (2005) examined a subset of the 14 most rigorous studies from both reviews. He found that the included interventions were moderately successful in increasing the proportion of securely attached children, and extremely successful in terms of achieving at least one specifically targeted therapeutic task. However, his findings suggested that it was not possible to produce a definitive answer as to whether 'less is more' or 'more is better' because *'less is more' for some, whereas 'more is better' for others* (Berlin 2005).

This points to the need to target interventions appropriately in terms of the specific needs of families, and of 'identifying and studying participants who vary with regard to key attachment processes' (Berlin 2005, p.20). For example, early findings suggest an association between adults' scores on a measure of attachment security and their responses to different types of psychotherapeutic intervention (e.g. parents classified as 'avoidant' were better suited to behavioural type interventions whereas parents classified as 'preoccupied' were better suited to interventions targeting internal working models) (Bakermans-Kranenburg, Juffer and van IJzendoorn 1998).

Strengths and limitations of the evidence about targeted interventions

Study designs

As with many other types of intervention, targeted programmes aimed at improving early indicators of emotionally insensitive parenting are often evaluated using non-randomized designs. Bakermans-Kranenburg, van IJzendoorn and Juffer (2003) found that out of 70 identified interventions only a small proportion had been evaluated using an RCT, and the more rigorous studies produced smaller effect sizes ($d = 0.36$ for RCTs cf. 0.61 for non-RCTs).

Study interventions

It can be difficult to get a clear picture from systematic reviews about what many of the 'attachment-based' interventions comprise. They are, however, wide-ranging, and it is an exciting time now to be working in the field, because there are numerous opportunities for practitioners to develop new skills in therapeutic work with families (see Chapter 9 for further detail).

Study populations

The populations in many included studies are often poorly defined. Most, however, clearly include parents who are demographically disadvantaged (e.g. FNP targets single, teenage parents), many of whom have also experienced extensive adversity in their own early parenting (e.g. unresolved trauma and abuse).

Study outcomes

The outcomes assessed in the included studies are diverse. For example, while home visiting programmes tend to focus on physical and behavioural outcomes, including maternal smoking and substance use, and early learning outcomes for the child, evaluations of interventions such as video-interaction guidance focus more explicitly on the assessment of maternal sensitivity and infant attachment security. One of the limitations of this literature is the lack of consistency across studies in terms of the measures used.

Many of the outcomes assessed comprise proxy measures of emotional maltreatment (i.e. they do not assess direct measures of abusive parenting), the most notable exception being the Nurse Family Partnership which now has effectiveness, cost, and 20-year follow-up data available, including an assessment of its impact on child abuse.

Summary

Targeting is a powerful means of focusing interventions where they are needed most and of ensuring that scarce financial resources are directed where they can produce most benefit. A range of factors have been used to date to identify eligible populations. This chapter suggests that alongside the use of demographic and clinical criteria, an assessment of parent–infant and parent–child interaction can be an effective means of targeting parents at risk of emotional maltreatment.

While there is, to date, limited long-term evidence concerning the effectiveness of early interventions in reducing the incidence of emotional maltreatment, there is, nevertheless, good evidence pointing to the benefits of a range of early interventions in terms of a number of proxy measures of emotional maltreatment, of which perhaps the best example is parental insensitivity. The evidence shows that interventions that target early parental insensitivity are effective in improving parenting behaviour and associated outcomes for children.

Section Three

Preventing the Recurrence of Emotional Maltreatment

5

Parent-Focused Interventions

Introduction

The next three chapters summarize the findings of our search to identify interventions aimed at preventing the *recurrence* of emotional maltreatment (see Figure 5.1). This chapter describes the *parent-focused* interventions that we identified. Parent-focused interventions are directed at the parent(s) only, and are aimed at changing some aspect of parental functioning (e.g. attitudes, beliefs or behaviour) and parental psychological wellbeing or mental health (e.g. anxiety and depression, anger).

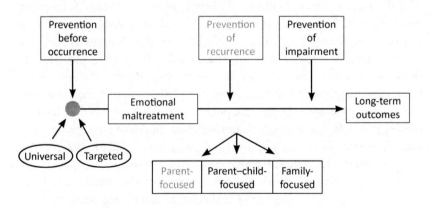

Figure 5.1 Focus of intervention

This chapter will address which parent-focused interventions have been evaluated, which appear to work and who they work best with, and will conclude with an exploration of the strengths and limitations of the evidence.

What interventions have been evaluated?

Parent-focused interventions are explicitly directed at changing some aspect of the parent's wellbeing or their parenting that is thought to contribute to emotionally abusive interactions with the child. Our search identified two key theoretical approaches underpinning parent-focused interventions – psychoanalytic and cognitive-behavioural – and these had been delivered using a range of formats (e.g. parenting and home visiting programmes). The following section briefly examines these theoretical approaches in terms of the aetiological model of abuse underpinning them, and the different treatment formats available, prior to examining the evidence about 'what works'.

Psychoanalytically informed approaches

Psychoanalytic theory posits that abuse results from parents' unconscious anger towards themselves, and towards their own parents, vented onto children (Steele and Pollack 1968). Selma Fraiberg *et al.* (1975) introduced the metaphor of 'ghosts in the nursery' to describe the ways in which parents re-enact with their children, their own unremembered but painfully influential childhood experiences of helplessness and fear. These 'ghosts' represent the repetition of the past in the present and express themselves as abusive or neglectful child-rearing practices. It is suggested that '(p)arents who have been traumatised can often find their children's needs and fears overwhelming and profoundly evocative, and as a result find it difficult to read the most basic cues without distortion or misattribution' (Lieberman 1997 cited in Slade *et al.* 2005, p.77). Indeed, as a result of their own unmet needs, maltreating parents may feel that they are 'in competition with their children for care and attention' (Baumrind 1994, p.361), and may seek from their children the care they did not receive (Main and Hesse 1990). Intervention is difficult because parents who have projected their own fear and anguish onto children often do not recognize that there is a problem, or present themselves as angry or concerned about the child but seeking assurance that the problem lies with the child (see Boulton and Hindle 2000).

A psychoanalytically informed approach to therapy thus focuses primarily on the mother's 'representational' world or the way in which the mother's current view of her child is affected by interfering representations from her own history, as expressed in the parent–therapist relationship. The aim of therapy is to help the mother to recognize the 'ghosts in the nursery' and to link them to her own past and current history, thereby facilitating new paths for growth and development for both mother and infant (Cramer and Stern 1988).

Cognitive-behavioural approaches

Cognitive-behavioural approaches to therapy are based on a combination of social learning theory and cognitive theory. Social learning theory proposes that human behaviour is governed by a system of costs and rewards and virtually all learning occurs on a vicarious basis by observing other people's behaviour and evaluating whether this has desirable outcomes (Bandura 1976). This theoretical framework purports that children are emotionally abused because parents have learned dysfunctional child-management practices (Iwaniec 2007).

Cognitive psychology, on the other hand, focuses on mental processes and in particular beliefs, desires and motivations, and their effects in terms of subsequent behaviour. Numerous studies have shown that parents who maltreat often 'tend to hold distorted beliefs and unrealistic expectations regarding the developmental capabilities of children, the age-appropriateness of child behaviours, and their own behaviour when interacting with children' (Sanders *et al.* 2004, p.515). Cognitive distortions of this nature can result in negative attributions of children's intentions and behaviour, as is the case, for example, when an infant's crying is perceived as an attack on the parent. Sanders *et al.* (2004) go on to observe that:

> these cognitive distortions have been linked to parents attributing hostile intent to their child's behaviour, which in turn has been linked with over-reactive and coercive parenting (Bugental 2000); angry feelings in parents (Slep and O'Leary 1998); child behaviour problems (ibid); and the use of harsh punishment (Azar 1997). (Sanders *et al.* 2004, p.515)

While many practitioners with a cognitive-behavioural orientation recognize that cognition is shaped by attachment and that a parent's experience of secure or insecure attachment influences their ability to read children's signals or interpret them correctly (Macdonald and Winkley 1999), cognitive-behavioural approaches are primarily concerned with changing parents' thoughts, beliefs and behaviour in the present, rather than analysing the role of past influences. Cognitive-behavioural approaches are wide-ranging but commonly focus on helping parents to change the way in which they perceive children, and the ways in which they interpret their own and their children's behaviour. These approaches help parents identify, confront and change their thinking, and develop better child-management skills. For example, such an approach will almost certainly involve challenging parental cognitions, assumptions, evaluations and beliefs that might be unhelpful and unrealistic, and will involve providing parents with alternative approaches to managing children's behaviour, and in particular to discipline. Cognitive-behavioural therapy (CBT) has been widely evaluated as an intervention approach with a range of mental health problems, and is now being recommended for use more widely (Department of Health 2009).

Delivery formats – individual and group-based interventions

Both cognitive-behavioural and psychotherapeutic approaches can be delivered on a one-to-one basis or to groups of clients. While the typical setting for the delivery of cognitive-behavioural and psychotherapeutic interventions has been on a one-to-one basis in clinics, the increasing trend towards the delivery of evidence-based and cost-effective interventions has led to the development of innovative group-based and individual formats (e.g. parent-training and home visiting programmes) for their delivery in the community. The next two sections provide further detail about these, before going on to examine the evidence about which parent-focused interventions work.

Parent-training programmes

Parent-training programmes are focused on enhancing parenting skills and changing parenting behaviours, and are underpinned by a range of theories in addition to CBT. Many were originally underpinned by social learning theory and, as such, incorporated a range of behaviour techniques aimed at helping parents to parent more effectively (e.g. encouraging the use of more effective child management techniques such as time-out strategies, points and rewards, etc.). The inclusion of cognitive-type approaches resulted in a shift of emphasis towards the use of problem-solving methods and strategies aimed at helping parents to address perceptions, attitudes and beliefs including distorted cognitions. More recently a number of attachment and mentalization-based parenting programmes have been developed (see Chapter 6 for further discussion).

Parent-training programmes can be delivered on a one-to-one basis in the home, or in clinics using bug-in-ear type strategies to give instructions to parents. They are also frequently delivered using groups, the Incredible Years series (www.incredibleyears.com) and Triple P (www.triplep.net) being possibly two of the best evaluated group-based programmes. (The Triple P Programme has a number of other formats as well – see Chapter 2). The methods used to deliver such programmes vary but typically involve the use of discussion, video vignettes and feedback, coaching, rehearsal and homework assignments.

One of the features that characterize parent-training programmes is the use of a manual and standardized format for their delivery. This means that while there is some scope to adapt the programme to meet the needs of individual clients (see Chapter 9 for further discussion), the content in terms of each meeting with the family is prescribed. Another feature of the most widely used parent-training programmes is that they require training to prepare practitioners for their delivery, and supervision of ongoing practice and delivery.

Parent-training programmes have been extensively evaluated and systematic reviews have shown them to improve parental psychosocial functioning (Barlow, Coren and Stewart-Brown 2002), and the treatment of child behaviour problems (Dretzke et al. 2009). There is also some evidence to suggest, however, that they do not work with all parents, and that significant numbers of parents in any group may not show benefit (Webster-Stratton and Hammond 1990). The question addressed by the studies that we identified is whether such programmes are effective in preventing the recurrence of emotional maltreatment.

Home visiting

Many groups of professionals visit clients in their home. However, like parenting programmes, standardized home visiting interventions typically involve the use of manualized and evidence-based ways of working with families. One of the best known and evaluated is the Nurse Family Partnership Programme which has been shown to be effective in preventing child abuse (Olds et al. 1998), and is currently being introduced across the UK (Rowe 2009). This programme involves intensive visiting of pregnant teenagers until their baby is two years of age, by specially trained home visitors. The programme is underpinned by ecological theory which emphasizes the importance of tackling a range of domains in terms of both the individual and their context (Bandura 1976), self-efficacy and attachment theory (see Chapter 6), and is aimed at improving outcomes for vulnerable pregnant women by:

1. helping them to improve their prenatal health-related behaviours including reducing cigarettes, alcohol and drugs, and identifying and obtaining treatment for emerging obstetric complications

2. improving the health of the infant postnatally by helping parents provide more responsible and competent care during the first year of life

3. improving parents economic self-sufficiency by helping them to develop a vision of the future, planning subsequent pregnancies, completing their education and finding work.

In order to do this, the nurses systematically involve fathers and other family members, and link families with other health and social services (Rowe 2009).

Home visiting has also been used, however, to deliver treatment programmes to families with older children, one example of such a programme being the Family Partnership Programme. This involved practitioners, who had been trained in the 'helping process' and methods of working in partnership and challenging parental constructions, to support families experiencing psychological problems (Davis and Spurr 1998) (see Chapter 9 for further detail).

A recent systematic review of reviews showed that while it is difficult to reach an overall conclusion regarding the effectiveness of such programmes (due in part to the diversity of their content, formats and providers), overall the evidence suggests that they are effective in improving a range of outcomes for children (Bull *et al.* 2004). The findings were, however, inconclusive in terms of their effectiveness in reducing abuse, and the question addressed by our review was whether there is evidence to show that such programmes are effective in preventing the recurrence of emotional maltreatment.

What parent-focused treatments work?

This section examines in more detail the explicit content of the parent-focused interventions that have been evaluated and the results in terms of their effectiveness in preventing the *recurrence* of emotional abuse.

Psychotherapeutic intervention approaches

We identified two good quality (evidence level A) evaluations of the effectiveness of group-based psychotherapeutic interventions combined with the use of home visits in the treatment of heroin-addicted mothers (Luthar and Suchman 2000; Luthar, Suchman and Altomare 2007). We included these because the classification of emotional maltreatment adopted for the purpose of this review defined drug abuse as being a form of missocialization, and a serious source of risk for emotional neglect. Both of the included studies assessed the impact of the intervention on the risk of child maltreatment and both were conducted in Australia.

One study compared the effectiveness of a clinic-based, weekly psychotherapy group – Relational Psychotherapy Mothers' Group (RPMG) – combined with a standard methadone treatment, with a standard methadone treatment alone for heroin-addicted mothers (Luthar and Suchman 2000). A more recent study involving a new, and larger sample, involved a comparison of the RPMG with cognitive-behavioural Recovery Training (RT) (Luthar *et al.* 2007). The cognitive-behavioural Recovery Training was conducted by professional clinicians with expertise in standard drug abuse treatment. It focused on processes of addiction and recovery and the reinforcement of skills aimed at preventing relapse into drug use.

Relational Psychotherapy Mothers Group

The Relational Psychotherapy Mothers' Group (RPMG) is a form of group psychotherapy aimed at facilitating optimal parenting among drug-addicted mothers. The intervention has four defining characteristics (Box 5.1). In the first 12 of 24 weekly sessions, RPMG addresses the mother's emotional vulnerabilities. The second 12 sessions focus on specific parenting issues.

Box 5.1 Defining features of RPMG

1. **Supportive therapist's stance:** Based on Rogerian constructs of acceptance, empathy and genuineness. This stance is viewed as essential to the fostering of a strong therapeutic alliance.

2. **Interpersonal relational focus:** Based on gender sensitive perspectives on women and interpersonal psychotherapy, this part of the intervention provides the basis for addressing the interpersonal isolation and stress of participating women, arising from their multiple roles, including that of parent.

3. **Group treatment to accommodate the chaotic schedules of many mothers; group membership is open or rotating:** Groups are led by female therapists, a female clinical psychologist and a female drug counsellor aimed at bringing therapeutic expertise across diverse domains including child development, women's psychology and addiction-related issues. The intervention is manualized, and all sessions are semi-structured.

4. **Insight-oriented parenting skill facilitation:** Participating women are encouraged to explore the strengths and limitations of their own strategies, and guided towards developing more optimal approaches via open-ended discussions, role plays and brainstorming exercises. This discovery-based, nondirective approach is aimed at empowering mothers, implicitly acknowledging their motivation to become better parents and their own capacities to foster the positive development of their families.

(Luther and Suchman 2000, pp.237–238)

Population

The first of the two studies (Luthar and Suchman 2000) compared the above Relational Psychotherapy Mothers Group with a standard methadone treatment control group, and involved 61 disadvantaged opiate-addicted mothers, of whom 10 per cent were African-American and 12 per cent Hispanic. The median age of the children was ten years. The more recent study (Luthar *et al.* 2007) involved 127 low socioeconomic status, opiate-addicted mothers, of whom 32 per cent were African-American and 12 per cent Hispanic. Most (85%) were receiving welfare, and 80 per cent were lone parents. Children had a mean age of nine years.

Outcomes for parents (see Appendix 2 for detailed reporting)

Both studies found that RPMG mothers reported robust and sustained improvements in affective interactions (i.e. warmth and acceptance) with children, and in their overall feelings of parental satisfaction post-treatment and at six-month follow-up. Both studies showed that while there was a trend towards improvement in depression for the RPMG group over those in the Recovery Training (study 2) or the control group (study 1) post-intervention, these effects were lost by six-month follow-up.

Both studies measured change in substance use based on computerized toxicology records at methadone clinics. Separate analyses were conducted for opiates (the primary drug for which women were in treatment) and for cocaine, commonly used by patients in methadone maintenance. The most recent of the two studies found that while the RPMG mothers' use of cocaine decreased over the course of treatment compared with that of the Recovery Training group (which increased over the same period), these gains were lost at six-month follow-up. The earlier study found that opiate use decreased over time in the RPMG group while it actually increased in the control group (i.e. that was receiving standard methadone treatment) over the same period, but that cocaine use decreased over the course of the year, with no difference between groups.

Outcomes for children

The study comparing RPMG with RT found improvements in RPMG mothers' reports of child maltreatment risk after the intervention, but these were lost after six months, with a significant decline in clinician-reported maternal functioning. In the earlier study that compared RPMG with standard methadone treatment, RPMG mothers showed significantly lower parent-and-child reports or risk of maltreatment. However, only parental reports of risk were still significant at the six-month follow-up.

Both studies measured children's psychosocial adjustment using a Parent Rating Scale (PRS) and a Self-Report Scale (SRP) for children aged 6 to 18. Although marginally significant differences were found in the personal maladjustment reported by children of RPMG mothers immediately post-treatment, no significant effects were found at six-month follow-up. No significant differences were found in mothers' reports of children's maladjustment either immediately after the intervention or at follow-up. While one study showed a reduction in the depression scores of children of RPMG mothers immediately post-treatment, these gains were lost six months post-treatment, when there were no longer any significant effects of RPMG children's depressive symptoms and an actual decline in the psychosocial adjustment of RPMG children.

Overall, while both of these studies found significant differences favouring the RPMG mothers post-intervention, most of these were seriously attenuated or had disappeared by the six-month follow-up. The authors suggest that while supportive parenting interventions of this nature for substance-abusing women appear to have some preventive potential, the abrupt cessation of the therapeutic programme may explain the poor longer-term outcomes.

Cognitive-behavioural parent-training

We identified two studies that had explicitly evaluated the effectiveness of cognitive-behavioural therapy (CBT) type approaches with emotionally abusive parents. One rigorous study (evidence level A) had examined the benefits of an enhanced family intervention underpinned by CBT (Sanders et al. 2004). A second less rigorous study (evidence level B) compared the potential benefits of CBT that was being delivered to emotionally abusive parents in a combined group and home-based format, with a home-based individual format alone (Iwaniec 1997a). One study was conducted in Australia, and the other in the UK.

The more recent of the two CBT-based studies evaluated the effectiveness of a standard group-based parent-training programme known as Triple P, with an enhanced programme including an adjunctive component designed to reduce anger and misattribution in parents reported for, or at self-reported risk of, emotional abuse (Sanders et al. 2004).

Triple P intervention

As was suggested in Chapter 3, the Triple P-Positive Parenting Programme is 'a multi-level, parenting and family support strategy that aims to prevent or reduce severe behavioural, emotional and developmental problems in children by enhancing the knowledge, skills and confidence of parents' (Sanders 1999, p.72). Triple P incorporates five levels of intervention of increasing strength for parents of children from birth to age 12.

- **Level 1** comprises a universal parent information strategy that provides parents with access to information about parenting through a coordinated media and promotional campaign using print and electronic media.

- **Level 2** comprises a brief, 1- or 2-session primary health care intervention providing anticipatory developmental guidance to parents of children with mild behaviour difficulties, with the aid of user-friendly parenting tip sheets and videotapes that demonstrate specific parenting strategies.

- **Level 3** comprises a 4-session primary care intervention, targeting children with mild to moderate behaviour difficulties and includes active skills training for parents.

- **Level 4** comprises an intensive 8- to 10-session individual, group or self-help parenting programme for parents of children with more severe behaviour difficulties.

- **Level 5** comprises an enhanced behavioural family intervention programme for families where parenting difficulties are complicated by other sources of family distress (e.g. relationship conflict, parental depression or high levels of stress).

The study that we identified compared the effectiveness of the Standard Behavioural Family Intervention (SBFI – Level 4 above) with an enhanced version called the Enhanced Behavioural Family Intervention (EBFI – Level 5 above). The EBFI incorporated additional sessions, and support focused on attributional retraining and anger management. These aimed to teach parents a variety of skills by challenging their beliefs with regard to their own and their children's behaviour, and to change negative practices underpinned by such beliefs. Parents were also introduced to a variety of physical, cognitive and planning strategies aimed at helping them to manage their anger including the concept of planning ahead in high risk situations (Sanders *et al.* 2004).

Population

The programme targeted 98 parents with a child aged two to seven years who had been referred by child protection services for emotional abuse (no further detail provided) or who had self-referred primarily because of concerns about their anger. The mean age of participating parents was 34 years and that of their children 4.4 years. The level of disadvantage of the parents was unspecified as were factors such as their ethnicity.

Outcomes for parents (see Appendix 2 for detailed reporting)

The study measured parental wellbeing and showed that parents in both groups had improved levels of anxiety and depression following the intervention. The study also found a significant decrease in both groups in parental distress and parental conflict, and in levels of anger associated with parenting (parental anger) and across life situations (global anger) for both versions of the programme. At the six-month follow-up parents who had taken part in the enhanced programme (EBFI) continued to improve at a greater rate in terms of anger management than those who had taken part in the standard programme (SBFI).

The study also measured a range of parenting attitudes and practices including parental blame and misattributions, unrealistic expectations, potential for child abuse, parenting style, parental satisfaction and efficacy. The results showed an improvement in parental blame and their attribution of children's intentions in both ambiguous and intentional situations for parents in both intervention groups. While immediately after the intervention, change was greatest for parents who had taken part in the enhanced version of the programme, by the six-month follow-up there was no significant difference between groups because parents who had taken part in the standard programme appeared to have 'caught up' with their counterparts in the enhanced programme.

The study also measured parents' unrealistic expectations of their children, showing that although both SBFI and EBFI groups had improved post-intervention and the strongest effects were for parents in the EBFI group, this difference had again disappeared by six-month follow-up because of continued improvements by parents in the standard intervention. A significant decrease was also found in parent reports of their potential for child abuse in both the enhanced and the standard versions, but again the stronger effects found in the enhanced version immediately after the intervention were no longer significant at six months due to the catch-up in the standard group.

Similar improvements were found after the intervention and at follow-up for parenting style, parental satisfaction and efficacy. There were similar levels of satisfaction with both interventions.

Outcomes for children

The authors of this study hypothesized that parents who took part in the enhanced programme would have significantly fewer notifications of child maltreatment at follow-up. This was not in fact the case and there were no differences in the number of notifications between the two groups – only one family had contact with the child protection services between the end of the intervention and six-month follow-up.

The study also used a number of measures to assess child emotional and behavioural wellbeing. Three different criteria were used to calculate reliable change post-intervention:

1. The Reliable Change Index (RCI) (Jacobson and Truax 1991).

2. A 30 per cent reduction in observed child disruptive behaviour (Webster-Stratton, Hollinsworth and Kapacoff 1989).

3. A normative comparison approach which involved calculating the proportion of children whose behaviour was normalized after the intervention (Barkley *et al.* 2001).

Reliable improvements were found in observed positive behaviour and reductions in observed negative behaviour of the children of participants in both groups, and there were no significant differences between the two groups in the number of children whose behaviour had improved or in the proportion of children in the non-clinical range. Parents in both groups reported a significant decrease in the number of parenting and child care situations in which they experienced problem behaviour both in the home and in the community. Assessment was also made of specific situations in the home (e.g. bedtime, getting dressed) and in the community (shopping, visiting friends) in which parents experience difficulties in managing their child's behaviour. Significant improvements were found in the management of these situations by parents in both groups, with no differences between them at follow-up.

Overall it is concluded that while at six-month follow-up both interventions showed similarly positive outcomes on all measures of child abuse potential, parent practices, parental adjustment and child behaviour and adjustment, only the EBFI group continued to show greater change in negative parental attributions. The authors suggest that this points to the benefits of delivering a less intensive intervention in the first instance, followed by reassessment to gauge whether there have been changes in the risk factors for maltreatment such as negative attributions, anger, coercive parenting practices and expectations, and that based on this assessment, customized adjunctive interventions targeting the specific risk factor should be offered.

Individual compared with group-based CBT programme

A second study compared a CBT-based parent-training programme delivered on a one-to-one basis in the home, with an enhanced programme involving the addition of ten group-based parent-training sessions aimed specifically at addressing factors that are strongly associated with abusive parenting (e.g. stress, problem-solving, etc.) (Iwaniec 1997a).

CBT intervention

The individual parent-training comprised ten weekly sessions of two hours duration and involved the development of a collaborative partnership with parents over the arrangement and agreements being made regarding the process and content of weekly sessions. The following topics were covered:

1. Developmental counselling in the form of discussions, clarifica-tions, instructions, advice and reassurance aimed at modifying parents' expectations.

2. Improving parent–child interactions and relationships through the exploration of parental attitudes and feelings about the child, and putting them into interactional contexts. Parents were shown graphically, using an ABC (antecedents, behaviour, consequences) analysis, how their behaviour and reactions influenced their children's behaviour, and were taught techniques to reduce ap-prehension and mutual avoidance behaviour, including structured interaction such as play and other activities that were increased over time. Some play sessions were videotaped and discussed.

3. Managing children's and parents' problematic behaviours involv-ing the introduction of specific and general child-rearing methods such as rules and boundaries, and the communication of these to children according to their developmental stage. Videotaped vignettes were used to demonstrate positive methods of reinforce-ment, and methods of dealing with difficult behaviour (e.g. time-out; correction; reasoning) were role-played, discussed and rehearsed (Iwaniec 1997a, pp.333–335).

Frequent telephone calls were made between sessions to support parents in the learning of new skills, provide advice, rehearse difficult tasks, and encourage and reinforce parental efforts.

The group-based parent-training comprised ten weekly sessions of two hours including a playgroup for the children and the transport of clients to sessions where appropriate. The programme focused on training in stress-management skills; self-control training; problem-solving abilities and the provision of a forum for mutual support, encouragement, exchange of ideas, etc. (Iwaniec 1997a, pp. 336–339).

Population

The study was undertaken with 34 emotionally abusive and neglectful parents with a median age of 25 years, referred by a paediatric assessment centre, outpatient clinics and local authority senior social workers. One-sixth of the sample was black and a similar proportion was single parents. Most families were of a low socioeconomic status.

Outcomes for parents (see Appendix 2 for detailed reporting)

The results showed significant reductions in the stress and anxiety levels of parents who received both the combined home- and group-based parent-training and those who received the home-based intervention alone. This study also measured parent's perception of the parent–child relationship before and after the intervention and found that more parents who received the combined intervention reported improvements in nine factors as a result of the intervention (46%, compared with 7% for the individual delivery alone group).

Outcomes for children

Observation of parent–child behaviours was undertaken by social workers to assess 22 forms of emotionally abusive behaviour (such as the child being ignored in the family circle, seldom being spoken to, socially isolated, not properly socialized and not permitted to show emotions). These behaviours were rated as occurring often, occasionally or almost never. Ratings for all behavioural goals were collapsed into the global categories of 'satisfac-tory/improved', 'moderately improved' and 'no improvement'. Both the combined treatment group (which received a combination of home-based and group-based parent-training), and the group that received home-based parent-training alone achieved statistically significant reductions in emo-tionally abusive behaviours. However, changes were more significant in the combined treatment group than in the home-based intervention alone. Before the intervention 99 per cent of participants in the combined treat-ment group said they were often emotionally abusive. By the end of the intervention, only 1 per cent of participants who received the combined home- and group-based treatment reported being emotionally abusive. In contrast, 88 per cent of parents in the group-based only treatment said they were emotionally abusive at baseline and 12 per cent continued to be emotionally abusive post-intervention.

Although no detail was provided about the number of reports of child maltreatment, the study found a greater reduction in children's highly negative, aversive reactions after the intervention in the combined treat-ment group. The author observes that these results are not wholly reliable because each child is affected in a different way by changes in their parents' behaviours.

Overall, this moderately rigorous study (evidence level B) suggests that both formats produced a range of improvements in emotionally abusive parenting, but that the additional group-based intervention resulted in significant improvements in areas other than child care.

Other parent-training programmes

We also identified a less rigorous pilot study (evidence level C) of the benefits of a client-centered, Adlerian and behavioural approach within two substance-abuse treatment programmes[3] (Knight, Bartholomew and Simpson 2007); and a retrospective follow-up study (evidence level D) assessing the benefits of the family nurturing programme on parenting attitudes and knowledge among inmates, and parents in substance abuse recovery populations (Palusci et al. 2008). These studies were conducted in the US.

Partners in Parenting

Partners in Parenting (PIP) was facilitated by two counsellors and sessions were provided twice weekly for two-hour sessions. The module ran for eight weeks. Group size averaged 12 and groups were 'closed' after two sessions (i.e. no further women were invited to participate in the group). Partners in Parenting focuses on parenting needs and goals; child development/parental expectations; age-appropriate communication, guidance and discipline strategies; and problem-solving (Box 5.2).

Population

The intervention was tested with 37 women who were admitted to the programme. Women were primarily Caucasian (white American) or African-American, over 24 years of age, and unmarried. Most had a high-school diploma and most were addicted to cocaine, cannabis or opiates other than heroin. Fifty per cent reported one or more arrests and 30 per cent current criminal justice status (e.g. on probation). Forty per cent reported having a child welfare case open. It should be noted that the outcomes reported below were obtained for only half of the women who took part in the programme.

Parent outcomes (see Appendix 2 for detailed reporting)

The study assessed the impact of the programme on the participating mothers in terms of parenting attitudes and behaviours, and family functioning.

---

3   We have reported the outcomes for the outpatient but not the residential group.

Box 5.2 Content of Partners in Parenting (PIP programme)

Session 1: Encourages participants to think about current parenting concerns and challenges, their goals and expectations for the sessions and the strengths and skills they bring to their role as parents.

Session 2: Focuses on child development principles, common parenting issues at different developmental stages and expectations of their children's behaviours.

Session 3 and 4: Focuses on family communication and techniques for conveying acceptance and emotional support through active listening skills. Speaking skills are also addressed as a strategy to help increase understanding and cooperation (e.g. importance of nonverbal communication and 'I-Messages' for communicating clearly about feelings and for setting limits and making requests.

Session 5 and 6: Highlights guidance and discipline issues; parents explore strategies such as the use of praise, reinforcement, setting limits, redirection and modelling. Ineffective methods of handling child behaviour are discussed alongside communication skills to provide child guidance. These sessions also introduce techniques such as ignoring, time-out and natural and logical consequences.

Session 7: Addresses issues of parent self-care including stress, insecurity and low self-efficacy. Parents are encourage to address their own needs and the negative impact of not doing so.

Session 8: Emphasises problem-solving, planning and encouraging resilience in children. It provides closure for the training and review of parenting goals that were set in the first session.

(Knight *et al.* 2007, pp.264–265)

Post-intervention, the study found non-significant improvements in around half of the items on a parenting attitude scale and in parenting behaviours for clients attending four or more sessions, including a significant reduction in inappropriate responses. Therefore, there were non-significant improvements in the amount of coercive discipline, use of clear instructions and encouragement. There were no improvements in two measures of family functioning.

Family Nurturing Programme – Helping Your Child Succeed (HYCS)

The Helping Your Child Succeed Programme is a modified version of the Family Nurturing Programme and is delivered to mixed groups of between 5 and 30 participants during structured 10–20-hour programmes using lectures, discussion and experiential learning. The programme is modelled on a family system approach and teaches 'democratic parenting techniques' (see Box 5.3) based on the belief that 'positive change in the parent must be attained before growth in the parent–child interaction can be achieved'. The average attendance was five to six classes (Palusci *et al.* 2008, p.81).

Box 5.3 Family Nurturing Programme: Helping Your Child Succeed (HYCS) – class topics

1. positive attention/praise
2. realistic and developmentally appropriate expectations
3. family rules/limit setting
4. personal power/negative control
5. managing anger
6. corporal punishment and alternatives
7. choices: natural and logical consequences
8. listening, communication and confrontation
9. communication and confrontation
10. assessment/seal the learning.

Population

This retrospective study reports data for 781 participants from a range of settings including incarcerated parents (substance abuse and batterers' programmes), residential drug treatment facilities, camps and community. The average age was 33 years, over half being male. Over 40 per cent reported minority race.

Parent outcomes

This retrospective study[4] examined the impact of the Family Nurturing Programme on parenting attitudes (e.g. expectations; empathy; corporal punishment; roles; independence), using the Adult Adolescent Parenting Inventory (APPI). The study found that all groups made significant gains in two or more (of five) scales, the highest gains being for the expectations, empathy and corporal punishment scales. Both genders made significant gains but males in all groups showed greater gain in parenting attitudes. Greater improvements were found in males with the highest baseline child abuse potential as measured by a parent-report instrument – the Child Abuse Potential Inventory (CAPI).

---

4   Data not reported in Appendix 2 due to the quality of the study.

Further examples of a cognitive-behavioural approach – case studies

Although we were only able to identify two studies that had evaluated the effectiveness of parent-focused interventions with emotionally abusive parents, we identified a number of further case studies (evidence level E) demonstrating the application of CBT techniques in work with a troubled dyad (Iwaniec 2007) and in the second case, with parents and their older children (Iwaniec 2007). These have been included as illustrations of this type of approach (i.e. not as evidence summaries).

Cognitive re-structuring, relaxation techniques and early prevention of abusive episodes

Cognitive treatment involves mapping thoughts by helping parents to identify 'cognitive distortions that are linked to thinking, feeling and behaviour that undermines the parent–child relationship' (Iwaniec 2007, p.263). In successive sessions, the parent is encouraged to challenge maladaptive thoughts and reward themselves for more adaptive ones. Alternative ways of thinking and behaving are suggested. For example, parents can be taught to conceptualize anger management as a state that is aggravated by self-presenting and often irrational thoughts, to identify 'triggers', and to 'interfere' with anger-provoking thoughts when these occur. 'Self-talk' ('My baby is not refusing to eat to annoy me, but because he is nervous and I can care for him'; 'this is not going to anger me') can help parents feel better and stall a potentially abusive episode. Potentially abusive episodes can also be stalled as parents learn how to apply relaxation techniques, including the use of relaxation tapes, and learning to detect (and respond to) physical feelings of tension and agitation. The onset of abusive episodes can also be prevented by enabling parents to identify which events 'trigger' particular difficulties.

The following case studies illustrate the principles of interventions that address 'parenting skills deficits', in which practitioners teach parents to use a range of cognitive and behavioural management strategies (Iwaniec and Herbert 1999).

REVERTING AVERSIVE MOTHER–INFANT INTERACTION

The intervention was undertaken with the mother of a 3½-year-old boy ('Jex') who had been born prematurely and who spent two months in intensive care. Jex was a 'difficult' baby for whom feeding, sleeping and general responsiveness presented problems. Jex's mother found it difficult to enjoy her child and feel that he belonged to her, despite her desire to do so. As time went on and he became more demanding, attention-seeking and antagonistic, her desire to love him had disappeared, and by the time he was 3½ years old they were mutually antagonistic. His mother's perception that Jex rejected her was exacerbated by the fact that Jex's 4½-year-old sister was a placid and easy child.

In addition to cognitive work, a variety of techniques were used to create greater physical and emotional proximity between Jex and his mother including 'story telling'. Although it was difficult for both mother and child to engage with or sustain physical contact, the mother was helped to initiate this and to read to Jex from picture story books. As the child's interest in the stories increased, he became less tense and his mother less anxious.

Following ten weeks of this type of intervention, the child expressed a sense of security by embracing his mother of his own accord, for the first time. From that point on, the relationship progressed rapidly and well.

(Iwaniec 2007, p.253)

Iwaniec describes a 'decision tree' that helps identify and define the problem, generate alternatives, consider the advantages and disadvantages of different courses of action, implement a plan, and review their progress and the success of the decision. These techniques can be combined and taught not only to parents, but also to older children.

Iwaniec (2007) also illustrates the application of a problem-solving approach to help a family in which both older siblings and parents verbally abused younger children and each other.

PROBLEM-SOLVING TRAINING FOR PARENTS OF OLDER CHILDREN

The 'Smith' family comprised a father, mother and seven children. Children were reported for emotional abuse and neglect. Interaction in the 'Smith' family was characterized by degrading and abusive language, not only by adults, but also by the three older children who bullied their younger siblings. One particular child had presented with chronic failure-to-thrive.

When faced with the possibility that Social Services might take the children into care, older children and parents engaged in a problem-solving approach to identify difficulties of mutual concern, brainstorm and look for a solution. Four issues were prioritized: (i) to cease verbal abuse, (ii) to establish clear and fair rules and routines, (iii) to establish times when the older girls could see friends, and (iv) for the father to reduce his alcohol consumption. Parents were also helped to identify 'trigger events' – sequences of events that led to negative emotional states and to avoid escalation of problems (e.g. by screaming at children). They learned to try to understand children's internal states and respond to the feeling in the child rather than screaming if, for example, a child destroyed a toy. The intervention took place over eight intensive sessions that were focused on working out problems and solutions (in the family home), and six follow-up/monitoring sessions. A practitioner co-ordinated the sessions, modelled techniques and provided feedback as the family tried out new behaviours. Parents were encouraged to use the decision tree (understand the causes of the situation, children's internal states, define their options, decide on an appropriate course of action and evaluate the effect of the action). Outcomes were evaluated at baseline and at one, two and six months and one year post-intervention. Cessation of verbal abuse and reduction of father's drinking were somewhat improved, while considerable improvement was noted at one year in the establishment of rules and routines, and the older children's respect of agreements about the times when they could see friends.

(Iwaniec 2007, pp.276–277)

It is suggested that behavioural interventions (in this case, behavioural social work) can enable parents (and children) to 'start over', and that focusing on the present and future may help parents who would otherwise be deterred from participating in programmes that they feel are 'blaming' them.

Home visiting

A further parent-focused approach is the use of intensive home visiting programmes. We identified one rigorous (evidence level A) (Dawe and Harnett 2007) and one pilot study[5] (evidence level C) (Dawe et al. 2003) evaluating the effectiveness of intensive home visiting programmes with methadone-maintained parents.[6] We also identified one rigorous study (evidence level A) (Black et al. 1995) evaluating the effectiveness of a lay home visiting programme, in addition to standard clinical services, for parents of children with faltering growth. We have also reported the findings of two follow-up evaluations of this intervention (Black et al. 2007; Hutcheson et al. 1997). These studies were conducted in Australia and the US.

---

5   This pilot study followed eight families at three months and found significant improvements in three domains: parental functioning, parent–child relationship, and parental substance use and risk behaviour. In addition to the changes in family functioning, the majority of families reported a decrease in concurrent alcohol use, HIV risk-taking behaviour and maintenance dose of methadone. The families reported high levels of satisfaction with the programme.

6   Harnett and Dawe (2008) has not been included because the type of abuse was not specified, and none of the participants was engaged with drug or alcohol treatment programmes.

Parents under Pressure (PUP)

The most recent of these studies evaluated the effectiveness of the Parents under Pressure (PUP) programme compared with a brief (two-session) traditional parent-training intervention and standard care (i.e. routine care by methadone clinic staff involving three-monthly meetings with the prescribing doctor and access to a case worker to assist in housing, employment and benefits). PUP is underpinned by an ecological model of child development and targets multiple domains of family functioning, including the psychological functioning of individuals in the family, parent–child relationships, and social contextual factors. The programme also incorporates 'mindfulness' skills that are aimed at improving parental affect regulation. PUP comprises an intensive, manualized, home-based intervention of ten modules conducted in the family home over 10 to 12 weeks, and each session lasting between one and two hours (Box 5.4).

Population

The randomized controlled trial (RCT) involved 64 methadone-dependent primary carers, 86 per cent of whom were mothers with at least one child aged between two and eight years in their full-time care. The mean age of the primary carers was 30 years, and mean duration in methadone treatment was 38 months, the mean daily dose of methadone being 62.5mg. Most families were in receipt of benefits payments (77%). The ethnicity of the parents was not specified.

Outcomes for parents (see Appendix 2 for detailed reporting)

Participants receiving the PUP programme showed significant reductions in parental stress and in methadone dose. There was also a significant reduction in child abuse potential as measured by the Child Abuse Potential Inventory (CAPI). Children of parents in the brief intervention showed a modest reduction in child abuse potential but no other changes. There was a significant worsening in the child abuse potential of parents receiving standard care.

Outcomes for children

Children of parents who received PUP showed significant improvements in child behaviour problems, and an increase in child prosocial scores. There were no improvements in the children of parents who received the brief intervention or standard care.

Overall, this study supports the growing body of research pointing to the importance of theoretically-based interventions that address multiple domains in families' lives, builds on their strengths, and addresses the individual risk profile of included families. It also points to the potential benefits of mindfulness-based techniques to improve parental affect.

Box 5.4 Parents under Pressure – module content

Module 1 and 2: Comprehensive family assessment; identification of targets for change.

Module 3: Challenging the notion of an ideal parent: aimed at strengthening the parents' perceptions of themselves as competent in the parenting role. Successes are added to a list of achievements in parent's workbook.

Module 4: How to parent under pressure: increasing mindful aware-ness. Teaches skills involved in coping with negative emotional states and mindfulness skills and techniques to tolerate negative emotional states without the need to avoid or escape them through the use of drugs.

Module 5: Connecting with your child and encouraging good behav-iour: teaches traditional behavioural skills including praise and reward to encourage good behaviour and child-centred play. Mindfulness techniques used to help parents focus on their children during play and increase their emotional availability.

Module 6: Mindful child management: teaches non-punitive child management techniques (e.g. time-out); mindfulness techniques include helping parents gain control over their own emotional respon-sivity in disciplinary situations aimed at reducing impulsive, emotion-driven punishment and increase the effectiveness of techniques taught in Module 5.

Module 7: Coping with lapse and relapse: teaches skills to minimize the risk of lapses, emphasizing prevention and mindful awareness of affective states that may be related to drug use such as craving.

Module 8: Extending social networks: encourages parents to extend their support networks through the identification of potential sources of support.

Module 9: Life skills: includes practical advice on diet and nutrition, budgeting, health care and exercise, etc. as needed.

Module 10: Relationships: aimed at improving effective communica-tion between partners and identifying past unproductive relationship patterns.

Lay home visiting programmes

The second home visiting study compared the effectiveness of adding a weekly trained lay home visiting service to standard clinic-based multidisci-plinary services (including hospital-based treatment of the child; hospital-based parent-training; and follow-up support from paediatricians, social workers and a community nurse). It assessed the effects at one year post-treatment (Black *et al.* 1995); when the children were within six months of their fourth birthday (Hutcheson *et al.* 1997); and at eight years of age (Black *et al.* 2007). The specially trained and experienced lay home visitors worked collaboratively with families to identify strengths, needs and priorities, and developed an individualized family service plan with specific goals and objectives (Box 5.5).

Box 5.5 Content of lay home visiting intervention

Theoretical model: Underpinned by an ecological model emphasizing the importance of a therapeutic alliance, the need to support the mothers' personal, family and environmental needs, and opportunities to model and promote healthy parent–child interaction and development, and the introduction of problem-solving strategies.

Curriculum guide: Based on the Hawaii Early Learning Programme to guide the parent–child interaction and child development phases of the intervention.

Materials: Personalized notebooks containing photographs of their children, calendars to record appointments and important events, handouts describing normal child development and age-appropriate activities. The notebooks were updated throughout the intervention. Home visitors used portable mats and toys to demonstrate developmentally appropriate activities and to facilitate parent–child interaction.

Number of visits: ranged from 0 to 47 with a mean of 19.2 with average length being one hour.

Integrity of intervention: Measured using personal contact record after each visit recording time spent, content and quality of the visit and goals and objectives for subsequent visits. Supervision by a community health nurse and weekly with a psychologist to track progress of families and intervention strategies.

(Black *et al.* 1995, p.809)

Population

This intervention was evaluated with 130 failure-to-thrive (FTT) infants with a median age of less than 18 months, and their predominantly disadvantaged, black, single mothers, of whom there were 76 in the three-year follow-up when the children were aged four (Hutcheson *et al.* 1997), and 47 at the eight-year follow-up (Black *et al.* 2007).

Outcomes for parents (see Appendix 2 for detailed reporting)

No significant changes were found in parental warmth and negative/non-negative status at the end of year one, and parents showed more control in their interactions with children during feeding, regardless of intervention status or children's age at recruitment. However, HOME (a measure of the home environment) scores indicated that children whose parents had received the combined lay home visitor intervention and clinic services had higher levels of parent–child interaction and nurturance, and lower negative control than those in the clinic-only control group.

Outcomes for children

The study found that children's weight for age and height, and height for age improved significantly after 12 months, irrespective of intervention group. Children who also received the lay home visiting intervention had better receptive language and a more child-oriented home environment than the clinic-only children. Younger children also showed benefits in terms of their cognitive development.

A further follow-up one year later when the children were nearly four years of age (Hutcheson et al. 1997) found that the intervention effects were mediated by the severity of the mothers' negative affect at baseline. At four years of age, the children of mothers with lower levels of negative affect showed improved cognitive development, motor development and child negativity during play. In contrast, higher rates of maternal negativity at baseline were associated with poorer outcomes for children's cognitive development and motor development and were marginally associated with poorer outcomes in children's task engagement. Levels of demographic risk (such as poverty and low levels of parental education) had no effect on outcomes either at the end of year one (Black et al. 1995) or by the time children were aged four (Hutcheson et al. 1997). In contrast, there was no difference in outcomes for children in the control group, irrespective of their mother's affect at baseline.

One final follow-up when the children were eight years of age (retention of 74–78% of the original sample) found no significant differences in IQ, reading or mother-reported behaviour problems, but fewer teacher-reported internalizing problems and better work habits in the home visiting compared with the clinical intervention-only group.

It is concluded from the follow-up at eight years that the home visiting 'attenuated some of the negative effects of early failure-to-thrive, possibly by promoting maternal sensitivity and helping children build strong work habits that enabled them to benefit from school' (Black et al. 2007, p.59). The follow-up of children at four years of age suggests that the intervention may be most effective with mothers who show low negative affectivity at the start of the intervention.

Residential treatment programmes

We identified two US studies evaluating the effectiveness of residential treatment programmes. The first was a one-group pre- and post-design (evidence level C) evaluating the effectiveness of a multimodal residential treatment programme for substance-abusing mothers (Conners *et al.* 2006), and the second was a residential version of the Parents in Partnership Programme (PIP) (see earlier in this chapter for a description of the intervention) (Knight *et al.* 2007).

Multimodal residential intervention

Arkansas CARES provides integrated services including daily substance abuse treatment; individual, group and family counselling and Twelve-Step meetings; parenting education and support; medical services; case management; support to education and employment; and aftercare. Children in treatment with their mothers receive a variety of educational and mental health services.

Population

Three hundred and five out of the 340 drug-using mothers who attended the Arkansas Centre for Addiction, Education and Services (Arkansas CARES) treatment programme between 2000 and 2004 were involved in the study. Two-thirds were Caucasian, 81.4 per cent single, with an average of two children of pre-school and school age. One-third was pregnant at the time of admission. Thirty-six per cent were at risk of severe depression, 51 per cent of post-traumatic stress disorder (PTSD) and 87 per cent had a previous history of arrest.

Parent outcomes (see Appendix 2 for detailed reporting)

Conners *et al.* (2006) used the Adult-Adolescent Parenting Inventory-2 (Bavolek and Keane 1999) to assess parenting and child-rearing attitudes of adult and adolescent parents. Significant improvements were noted on the parent–child role reversal (parentification) subscale, with more significant results for longer length of stay, and in the inappropriate expectations subscale, which were marginally associated with length of stay. Significant improvements were also found for the total scale pre- to post-intervention.

Conners *et al.* (2006) also found a significant reduction in depressive symptoms from intake to follow-up, with better outcomes associated with longer length of stay in the residential treatment programme, and significant improvements in symptoms associated with PTSD, although this was not linked with length of stay. No significant effect was found on empathy, promotion of children's autonomy or belief in the use of corporal punishment.

Just under half of participants reported being completely abstinent from alcohol or illicit drugs in the period between discharge and assessment with longer stays associated with increased abstinence. There was also a significant reduction in cigarette use, also associated with length of stay, significant changes in needle use, lower rates of arrest and marginal reductions in risky sexual behaviour. There was no relationship between length of stay and needle use, a strong association between length of stay and rates of arrest, and a marginal association between length of stay and risky sexual behaviour.

The study also found a significant increase in clients' employment after treatment, associated with longer length of stay, and there was a small but significant increase in the number of clients living above the poverty line from intake to final assessment, also associated with increased length of stay. The number of clients living independently increased after discharge but was not associated with length of stay.

Knight *et al.* (2007) also report outcomes on a 16-item parenting attitude scale for 24 substance-abusing mothers. The results show significant improvements for four items and large non-significant improvements in six further items.

Overall, these studies provide preliminary evidence to suggest that intensive multimodal residential treatment programmes that incorporate a parenting component are effective in improving parenting attitudes and behaviour.

Strengths and limitations of the evidence about parent-focused treatments

Study designs

Only a small number of the included studies met the gold standard in terms of being randomized controlled trials. However, all of the included RCTs compared two active treatments (e.g. standard and enhanced Triple P programmes). This is acceptable where the benefit of an intervention has already been demonstrated using a control group (e.g. Triple P), but this was not the case for most of the included studies.

Study interventions

The included studies comprised a mix of theoretical approaches (cognitive; psychotherapeutic; ecological), delivery formats (parent-training; group;

home visiting), and providers (professionals and non-professionals), and the interventions were delivered to a variety of study populations (see below). None of the studies compared different theoretical approaches (see next chapter for further discussion), and although there was some attempt in some studies to compare delivery formats (e.g. one-to-one versus group), it was often not possible as a result of the design of the study to ascertain the effective component of an intervention. For example, one study compared a group- and home-based CBT programme with a home-based programme alone (Iwaniec 1997a). While the combined intervention was found to be more effective, the design of this study precluded the possibility of assessing whether the group-based or home-based components of the intervention were the active ingredient. Similarly, an evaluation of the PUP programme appeared to suggest the value of a mindfulness component targeting negative parental affect, but the study design precluded the possibility of demonstrating this (Dawe and Harnett 2007).

Study populations

Some of the included studies had explicit criteria in terms of eligibility (e.g. current drug abuse), but the small number of studies that had included parents defined as 'emotionally abusive' all failed to make explicit the criteria used to diagnose and select parents. For example, one study involved parents identified as emotionally abusive by child protection services without further detail (Sanders et al. 2004). At least half of the sample in this study had self-referred because of concerns about their anger. The intervention thus included a substantial proportion of participants who were aware of their difficulties in managing anger. It has been suggested that parents who are severely abusive are unlikely to self-refer, precisely because of their extreme cognitive distortions, and that such parents are more likely to blame the child(ren) for their externalizing behaviours (Boulton and Hindle 2000). Thus, while a proportion of the parents in this sample had been formally diagnosed as emotionally abusive, it seems unlikely that the group included a majority of parents with the severe psychopathology identified in some of the other included studies. Similarly, the second study that included emotionally abusive parents also failed to provide any further detail with regard to the nature of the abuse, although it is clear that the sample were all severely disadvantaged (Iwaniec 1997a).

Study outcomes

The limitations of the included studies in terms of the outcomes is that most had used proxy measures of emotional abuse, such as parental functioning (e.g. misattributions or anger) or child reports of abuse or wellbeing. Very little assessment was made of more objective measures of abuse, such as the number of children who were the subject of a child protection plan, and although one study included direct observations of parent–child interaction, this was undertaken using a non-standardized instrument designed specifically for the study.

Summary

The evidence about the effectiveness of parent-focused interventions to prevent the recurrence of emotional abuse is complex because it covers a range of different ways of working (i.e. cognitive-behavioural approaches, both individual and group-based; psychotherapeutic; and home visiting), with diverse groups of parents, whose parenting is failing to meet the emotional needs of their children (i.e. parents diagnosed as emotionally abusive; drug-abusing parents; and parents of children diagnosed with faltering growth). Despite the limitations of the evidence, the findings suggest a number of implications for practice in terms of the use of *parent-focused* interventions for emotionally abusive parents.

The research points to the *potential* value of providing CBT-based interventions to emotionally abusive parents. The rigorous evaluation of the Triple P Programme, for example, added yet further evidence of the benefits of this wide-ranging approach. Our main concern related to the fact that some of the population were at the less severe end of the spectrum in terms of their presenting problems. A second less rigorous study also showed the benefits of using CBT-based techniques on a one-to-one and combined individual and group basis.

The findings also suggest the potential value of adjunctive components that are specifically aimed at addressing factors known to be associated with emotionally abusive parenting. For example, one study assessed the added value of additional anger management and attributional retraining (Sanders *et al.* 2004), another assessed the benefits of group-based components targeting parental functioning (e.g. stress and problem-solving training) (Iwaniec 1997a) and a further study explicitly incorporated 'mindfulness' techniques aimed at improving negative parental affect (Dawe and Harnett 2007). All of these studies showed beneficial outcomes for families, even though it was not always possible to demonstrate explicitly the value of the additional component (except in the case of the Triple P Programme).

We also identified some innovative ways of working with drug-abusing parents that were explicitly aimed at reducing the risk of child abuse and improving parenting. These included a developmentally informed, supportive psychotherapy group (Relational Psychotherapy Mothers Group), and an intensive, ecologically-based and multifaceted intervention (Parents under

Pressure programme) targeting a number of domains of family functioning, in addition to standard methadone support. It is notoriously difficult to improve outcomes for drug-abusing families and, to date, there have been limited attempts at explicitly improving parenting. RPMG capitalized on the desire of isolated, addicted women for affiliation. The follow-up at six months of a second evaluation of this intervention, however, found no long-term benefits (Luthar *et al.* 2007). The authors concluded that women may have become more aware of what was missing in the deprived urban environment in which they conduct their everyday lives and experienced increased levels of distress as a result. As Steele and Pollack (1968, p.141) observed: 'Termination of treatment can arouse once more the feelings of being deserted and rejected, and not rarely there will be a mild transient recurrence of tendencies to demand too much and be too aggressive towards the infant.' It is possible that support groups of this nature would be more effective if they were long term and grounded in community-based, naturally occurring settings, in which new attachments could be created and sustained.

Both RPMG and PUP are underpinned by sound theoretical principles, and as Dawe and Harnett (2007) have observed, such interventions need to address the multiple domains of families' lives. They also point to the importance of building an individual risk profile for each family.

6

Parent–Child-Focused Interventions

Introduction

This chapter examines the findings of our search to identify parent–child focused interventions (Figure 6.1) that are aimed at preventing the *recurrence* of emotional abuse. Parent–child-focused interventions are directed explicitly at the parent–child dyad, and are aimed at changing some aspect of parental functioning (e.g. attitudes, beliefs or behaviour) or parental well-being, such as mental health (e.g. anxiety and depression, anger) or both by targeting the relationship between the parent and child.

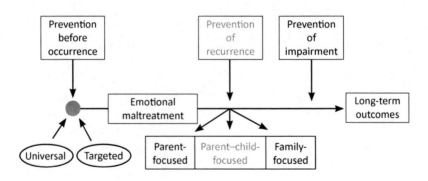

Figure 6.1 Focus of intervention

The chapter will address which parent–child-focused interventions have been evaluated, which appear to work and who they work best with, and will conclude with an exploration of the strengths and limitations of the evidence.

What interventions have been evaluated?

Parent–child-focused treatments involve interventions that are explicitly directed at changing some aspect of parent–child interactions that is thought to contribute to the emotional abuse of the child. Our search identified three key theoretical approaches underpinning parent–child-focused interventions – psychoanalytic, attachment, and mentalization. The following section examines these treatments in more detail prior to examining the evidence about 'what works'.

Psychoanalytically informed interventions

Psychoanalytical theory has informed a number of interventions for parents, and the work of a number of notable researchers during the latter part of the last century (e.g. Fraiberg 1980; Stern 1998) led to the development of *dyadic* therapies that involve working simultaneously with both the parent and the infant or child. The earliest approach, developed by Selma Fraiberg (1980), focused primarily on the mother's 'representational' world ('representation-focused' approach) or the way in which the mother's current view of her infant is affected by interfering representations from her own history. The aim of therapy is to help the mother to recognize the 'ghosts in the nursery' and to link them to her own past and current history, thereby facilitating new paths for growth and development for both mother and infant (Cramer and Stern 1988). One of the basic objectives of dyadic psychotherapies is to focus also on the current interaction between parent and child to gain an understanding of the 'influences of maternal representation on parenting as maternal representations and distortions are enacted within the context of preschooler–parent interactions' (Toth *et al.* 2002, p.891). The therapy is used to explore the parent's history and to promote understanding of the links between this and their current parenting, within the context of a corrective emotional experience between parent and therapist (see Box 6.2).

Box 6.1 Parent–infant psychotherapy

Maltreating mothers, who often have childhood histories of disturbed parent–child relationships and frequent negative experiences with social services systems, often expect rejection, abandonment, criticism and ridicule. Through empathy, respect, concern, and unfailing positive regard, therapists help maltreating mothers to overcome these negative expectations and provide a holding environment for the mother and preschooler in which new experiences of self in relationship to others and to the preschooler may be internalised. (Toth *et al.* 2002, p.891)

Box 6.2 Attachment

Bowlby argued that infants are born with a repertoire of behaviors (attachment behaviors) aimed at seeking and maintaining proximity to supportive others (attachment figures). In his view, proximity seeking is an inborn affect-regulation device (primary attachment strategy) designed to protect an individual from physical and psychological threats and to alleviate distress. Bowlby (1988) claimed that the successful accomplishment of these affect-regulation functions results in a sense of attachment security – a sense that the world is a safe place, that one can rely on protective others, and that one can therefore confidently explore the environment and engage effectively with other people. (Mikulincer, Shaver and Pereg 2003, p.78)

Recent interventions have combined representational and behavioural approaches (Cohen *et al.* 1999). For example, 'Watch, Wait and Wonder' (see Box 4.1) is an infant/toddler-led parent–infant psychotherapy which involves the mother spending time observing her child's self-initiated activity, accepting their spontaneous and undirected behaviour, and being physically accessible to the child. The mother then discusses her experiences of the play with the therapist with a view to examining the mother's internal working models of herself in relation to her child (Cohen *et al.* 1999).

There is a growing body of evidence pointing to the effectiveness of parent–infant psychotherapy (Cohen *et al.* 2000). There is also evidence suggesting that different forms of the therapy may be differentially effective for parents with different types of attachment insecurity (Bakermans-Kranenburg *et al.* 1998).

Attachment-based interventions

The central aim of attachment-based interventions is to improve the sensitivity of the parent to the emotional needs of the child, and in particular to their needs at times of distress, fear and threat. Most attachment-based interventions are aimed at promoting secure infant attachment. Attachment refers to an instinctual, two-way process by which infants use genetically inherited skills, such as smiling, grasping and crying, to create a bond between mother and baby, which prompts the mother to meet the infant's need for protection, food and nurture (Bowlby 1988) (see Box 6.2).

Attachment is thus recognized to be a core component in the process by which a child begins to be able to recognize and regulate their emotions, and this begins with the infant gradually developing trust and understanding, as a result of the predictable and reliably attuned responses of their caregiver (Howe 2005).

The importance of the attuned responsiveness of caregivers is that children build an *internal working model* of early interactions – 'a model that best fits the reality that he or she experiences as the child grows older' (Baumrind 1994, p.366). Mikulincer *et al.* (2003) write regarding this:

> Interactions with significant others who are available in times of need, sensitive to one's attachment needs, and responsive to one's bids for proximity [attachment-figure availability] facilitate the optimal functioning of the system and promote the formation of a sense of attachment security. As a result, positive expectations about others' availability and positive views of the self as competent and valued are formed, and major affect-regulation strategies are organized around these positive beliefs. However, when significant others are unavailable or unresponsive to one's needs, proximity seeking fails to relieve distress, and a sense of attachment security is not attained. As a result, negative representations of self and others are formed (e.g. worries about others' good will and doubts about self-worth), and strategies of affect regulation other than proximity seeking are developed [secondary attachment strategies]. In other words, attachment-figure availability is one of the major sources of variation in strategies of affect regulation. (Mikulincer *et al.* 2003, p.79)

An infant who experiences a cold, detached response from a primary carer (for example, when crying for help) may develop an attachment style that shuns making demands or intimacy with others. As the recipient of the parent's negative attributions, the child comes to internalize a sense of self as unworthy and undeserving of love.

When the source of danger is the carer (typically a maltreating parent) 'children's attachment behaviour becomes increasingly incoherent and disorganised, showing a mixture of avoidance, anger, disorientation and inertia' (Howe *et al.* 1999, p.29). In their observations of mothers and infants, Main and Hesse (1990) identified a series of actively hostile, frightening and frightened behaviours by mothers that they called 'atypical' or 'Fr-behaviour'. These behaviours can be subtle (for example, periods of being dazed and unresponsive) or more overt (deliberately frightening children). Several instruments have been developed to measure parents' engagement in these behaviours. A coding system introduced by Main and Hesse (1992) to assess Fr-behaviour has been developed by others, and has shown a strong association between Fr-behaviour and maternal unresolved loss (Jacobvitz *et al.* 1997). Research by Jacobovitz *et al.* (1997) suggests that Fr-behaviours are distinct from neglect and express a distorted image of the child, which is the consequence of the mother's unresolved trauma and losses.

Attachment-based interventions are diverse because the aim of improving attachment can be incorporated within very different models of intervention, some of which are underpinned by behavioural strategies (i.e. aimed at improving maternal sensitivity by altering maternal behaviours) and others by more psychotherapeutic approaches (i.e. aimed at improving maternal sensitivity by altering maternal representations). They can also be delivered using diverse formats ranging, for example, from the use of infant carriers to more complex formats such as home visiting programmes (for example, see Bakermans-Kranenburg *et al.* 1995).

Interaction guidance is a 'behavioural' approach that involves the use of videotaped interactions of mother and infant by the therapist to help the mother to recognize her own positive responses and interactions with her infant, and to elaborate appropriate responsiveness. Mutual enjoyment and pleasurable interactions are identified and encouraged with a view to building maternal confidence (McDonough 2000).

Mentalization-based parenting programmes

Mentalization-based programmes are an emerging model of intervention that build on recent advances in attachment theory. Mentalization-based therapies (Bateman and Fonagy 2004) have been developed over the past few years and involve treatments that directly address and target the development of reflective functioning or mentalising capacities (Bateman and Fonagy 2004). Mentalization refers to the capacity to 'envision mental states in the self and other' (Slade *et al.* 2005, p.76), and its importance in terms of child development is that children need to learn about their own mental states and those of others. They do this primarily as a result of their early interaction with parents who are able to 'mentalize' or whose 'reflective capacity' is such that they are able to identify and contain the child's early emotional states and fears. This involves parents being able to see their baby as 'intentional' rather than as a collection of physical and behavioural states only. It is suggested that mentalization is essential to affect modulation and that 'regulation experiences that can be known and understood, held in mind without defensive distortion can be integrated and contained' (Slade *et al.* 2005, p.76). Recent research showed that a mother's capacity to interpret her baby's moods or feelings was a better predictor of child development at two years of age, than the mother's income or educational status (Meins *et al.* 2002).

Applied to parenting, mentalization-based approaches involve enabling parents to understand their child as an intentional being, and have informed the development of new parenting programmes that are aptly named 'Minding the Baby'. This comprises a combination of nurse home visiting (see Chapter 5 for further details) and infant–parent psychotherapy (see above), and is directed at highly traumatized mothers and infants, with the aim of 'addressing the particular relationship disruptions that stem from mothers' early trauma and derailed attachment history' (Slade *et al.* 2005, p.75).

Which interventions work?
Psychoanalytic approaches
We identified two studies (evidence level A) evaluating the effectiveness of a parent–child psychotherapy intervention for emotionally abusive parents (Cicchetti, Rogosch and Toth 2006; Toth *et al.* 2002) and one further study (evidence level A) evaluating the effectiveness of a similar intervention with mothers with major depressive disorder (Toth *et al.* 2006). We also identified one case series (evidence level E) exploring the application of mother–infant group psychotherapy with substance abusing mothers (Belt and Punamaki 2007). The first three studies were conducted in the US and the fourth in Israel.

Parent–infant/toddler psychotherapy
These first two studies (Cicchetti *et al.* 2006; Toth *et al.* 2002) involved the evaluation of an infant–parent (IPP) and Preschooler–Parent Psychotherapy (PPP) intervention respectively focusing on the mother's interactional history and the effect that this has on representations of her child. In the first study (Cicchetti *et al.* 2006) mother and infant met weekly with a therapist at home over the course of one year. The approach is supportive, nondirective and nondidactic, and includes developmental guidance based on the mother's concerns. During the session, the mother and therapist jointly observe the infant, and the therapist aims to 'allow distorted emotional reactions and perceptions of the infant as they are enacted during mother–infant interaction to be associated with memories and affects from the mother's prior childhood experiences. Through respect, empathic concern and unfailing positive regard, the therapeutic relationship provides the mother with a corrective emotional experience, through which the mother is able to differentiate current from past relationships, form positive internal representations of herself and of herself in relationship to others, particularly her infant. As a result of this process, mothers are able to expand their responsiveness, sensitivity and attunement to the infant, fostering security in the mother–child relationship and promoting emerging autonomy

in the child' (Cicchetti *et al.* 2006, pp.629–630). This intervention was compared with a preventive home-based education programme focused on infant physical and psychological development and parenting, encouraging mothers to seek further education and employment, and the provision of enhanced informal social support (PPI), and a standard community control group (CS).

In the second study (Toth *et al.* 2002) mothers and preschoolers were seen weekly for 60 minutes in a clinic, and a number of periodic home visits were also offered. Therapy similarly focused on helping the mother recognize how her past history was re-enacted in the present, and enabling her to change her representations. This intervention was compared with a CBT-based psychoeducational home visitation programme (HVP) focused on parenting skills training, and a standard community services programme (CS) for maltreated preschoolers and their mothers.

Population

The first study sample comprised 137 one-year-old infants from maltreating families and their mothers (aged 18 to 41 years). The majority (74%) were of minority race/ethnicity. Six hundred and ninety-five of the infants had been emotionally abused, 85 per cent had been neglected and 9 per cent had been physically abused.

The second study sample comprised 87 mothers and their preschool infants. All of the children in the sample had experienced a number of combinations of different types of abuse, and one-third had been diagnosed as suffering emotional abuse only or emotional abuse and neglect. Sixty-five per cent of the sample comprised minority ethnic groups, and all were disadvantaged.

Parent outcomes (see Appendix 2 for detailed reporting)

Cicchetti *et al.* (2006) did not assess parent outcomes. Toth *et al.* (2002) showed a significant decrease in maladaptive maternal representations post-treatment in the PPP group but not in the PHV or CS conditions.

Child Outcomes

In the first study (Cicchetti *et al.* 2006) children in the IPP (61%) and PPI (55%) groups demonstrated substantial increases in secure attachment. There were no increases in secure attachments in the CS group. Significantly few infants in the IPP (32%) and PPI (46%) groups were classified as disorganized post-intervention.

In the second study (Toth *et al.* 2002) children's narratives were used to assess change in maternal and child representations pre- and post-intervention. The authors used 11 'Story Stems' (selected from the MacArthur Story

Stem Battery (MSSB) (Bretherton *et al.* 1990) and the Attachment Story Completion Task (Bretherton, Ridgeway and Cassidy 1990). An abbreviated version of the Wechsler short form (WPPSI-R) was used to measure intellectual functioning of children aged three to seven. The study found that although children in all four conditions – preschooler–parent psychotherapy (PPP), psychoeducational home visiting (PHV), community standard (CS) intervention and no-treatment controls – exhibited more positive expectations of the mother–child relationship over the period of observation, the most dramatic improvements were found in preschoolers whose mothers were in the PPP group. These dyads had received the lowest mother–child relationship score at baseline and the highest at post-intervention assessment. The study also found a significant post-intervention difference in the positive self-representations of children in the PPP and CS groups. Only a marginal increase was found in the PHV group.

Overall, it is concluded that this model of intervention is more effective at improving representations of self and of caregivers than a didactic model of intervention directed at parenting skills. One of the key problems with this study, however, is the limited outcomes examined (see below for further discussion).

Toddler–parent psychotherapy

The second study of a toddler–parent psychotherapy intervention (Toth *et al.* 2006) with mothers with major depressive disorder focused on reorganizing attachment in the offspring of these mothers. The principles of the intervention were similar to Toth *et al.* (2002) above. Mother–toddler dyads received an average of 45 weekly one-to-one sessions. It is suggested that 'therapeutic change thus occurs through expansion of maternal understanding of the effects of prior relationships on current feelings and interactions. Through the development of more positive representational models of self and of self in relation to others, improvements in maternal sensitivity, responsivity, and attunement to the child are found to increase' (Toth *et al.* 2006, p.891).

Population

The sample comprised 130 mothers who had experienced a major depressive episode some time since the birth of their child. They ranged in age from 21 to 41 years and their children were on average 20.34 months of age. Families were not of low socioeconomic status (i.e. not receiving public assistance) and were required to have at least high school education. The mothers were predominantly European/American (93%) and were mostly married (88%).

Maternal outcomes

There were no observed effects on maternal subsequent depressive episodes or on the severity of the episodes.

Toddler outcomes

Post-intervention the percentage of secure attachments in the intervention group was significantly higher than in the depressed control group (p<0.001), and also higher than a non-depressed control group (p<0.04). The percentage of disorganized attachments was also significantly lower in the intervention group than in the depressed control group (p<0.001).

Overall, it is concluded that these results demonstrate the efficacy of toddler–parent psychotherapy in fostering secure attachment relationships in young children of depressed mothers.

Mother–infant group psychotherapy intervention

We also identified one paper exploring through the use of a series of case studies the application of a method of outpatient care comprising a brief (20 to 24 three-hour sessions over six months – pregnancy to postpartum), dynamic mother–infant group psychotherapy with substance-abusing mothers (Belt and Punamaki 2007). The core therapeutic elements of the model include the group providing a 'symbolic maternal lap, and the meeting of the mothers' and the infants' need...' in the hope that this may offer the mothers 'a new experience within which to reappraise their early memories' thereby preventing them from 'projecting traumatic past experiences onto their infants' (Belt and Punamaki 2007, p.202). The box below provides some clinical vignettes demonstrating the work undertaken.

The authors conclude that 'brief dynamic mother–infant group psychotherapy seems to be a promising form of treatment for those substance-abusing women able to commit to outpatient care and examine the causes of their drug dependence' (Belt and Punamaki 2007, p.202), but rigorous evaluation of this approach is now needed.

Attachment-based approaches

We identified one moderately rigorous Canadian study that had evaluated the effectiveness of interaction guidance (evidence level B) (Benoit *et al.* 2001), and one less rigorous study (evidence level C) of its use with parents with severe mental illness (Pawlby *et al.* 2005). We have also included in this section a one-group evaluation (evidence level C) of the effectiveness of a video-based intervention entitled Circle of Security (Hoffman *et al.* 2005), although it should be noted that while the intervention population are high risk of poor outcomes, it is not clear that they meet current criteria of being emotionally abusive (i.e. a minority are described as having maltreated their children).

Box 6.3 Clinical vignettes

Mary is angry, demands a lot of attention from the therapists and ignores her baby. The therapists try to calm her down and ask her to tell them what has happened. She describes how her baby's fingers had clung to her hair at home, and how it caused a strong reaction in her: 'I lost my temper and I remembered how my mother dragged me by the hair with my feet 10cm from the ground. I left the baby crying and I went to the balcony for a cigarette to calm my nerves...'

Linda always feeds her baby with unheated milk. During lunch we discuss the memories that the mothers have of food when they were little children. Linda finds a connection between the cold bottle and her childhood experience. She remembers how her own mother and baby-sitter forced her to eat and drink food and liquids so hot that her mouth was burned over and over again.

Julia is a four-month-old baby girl, whose mother Ann is neglecting her needs. Even in the winter in the freezing cold, Ann dresses Julia lightly and gives her too little milk from a dirty feeding bottle. Ann is always very hungry and greedily eats the food that is served in the group. In the first sessions the therapists allow her to concentrate on her own needs, but gradually they and group members express their worry about the adequacy of Julia's feeding and the warmth of her clothing. The thera-pists make a whole group interpretation of the mother–infant ravenous hunger and unsatisfied need, and how Ann very clearly expresses group members' hunger for the group's care. Other members of the group have already discreetly taken responsibility for the situation. In the following session one of the mothers brings her own baby's nice warm clothes for Ann, who proudly puts them on Julia. The other mothers show how they prepare milk and gauge their babies' hunger. Ann feels that the group has understood her and appreciate her, and she accepts the advice. She soon dresses Julia warmly, gives her more food and holds her more closely. Gradually, Julia's weight increases, and her interaction with Ann becomes more active, to the extent that Ann complains that she gets tired of Julia's liveliness. (Belt and Punamaki 2007, pp.209–210)

Interaction guidance

Intervention

The first study (Benoit *et al.* 2001) involved interaction guidance that consisted of 90-minute sessions – approximately 15 minutes of videotaped interaction followed by 75 minutes of discussion, education and feedback – administered over five consecutive weeks. The intervention included an individually tailored information component on specific issues exhibited by the infant. This intervention was compared with a behavioural feeding programme.

Population

The sample comprised 28 infants diagnosed with faltering growth and their mothers. The median age of the mothers was 32 years and 18 months for the infants. Just under half of the sample was from disadvantaged social groups. Ethnicity was not specified.

Parent outcomes (see Appendix 2 for detailed reporting)

This study used the Atypical Maternal Behavior Instrument for Assessment and Classification (AMBIANCE) (Bronfman *et al.* 1999) to code the following atypical maternal behaviours during one minute of play interaction:

1. Affective communication errors.

2. Role reversal.

3. Frightening/disoriented behaviour.

4. Intrusiveness and negative behaviour.

5. Withdrawal.

A summary score is obtained by adding up the scores for each of these five categories. This includes a qualitative score for level of disrupted communication and a bivariate classification for disrupted or non-disrupted communication. This study focused primarily on global measures of change in parenting behaviour.

A significant decrease in disrupted communication was found between mothers and infants from pre- to post-intervention in the Interaction Guidance group, in contrast with the feeding-focused group which remained stable. In the pre-intervention session, 85 per cent of the mothers in the Interaction Guidance group and 43 per cent of those in the feeding-focused group were classified as 'disrupted', while 15 per cent of the mothers in the Interaction Guidance group and 57 per cent of those in the feeding-focused group were 'non-disrupted'. Those in the Interaction Guidance group were significantly more likely to attain a classification of 'non-disrupted' by the end of the intervention than the feeding-focused group.

It is concluded that this study provides preliminary evidence of the effectiveness of interaction guidance, although the outcomes measured were, once again, very limited.

A second study evaluated the benefits of video-interaction guidance with mothers diagnosed as having severe mental illness (Pawlby *et al.* 2005).

Circle of Security

One study evaluated the effectiveness of the Circle of Security Intervention (Hoffman *et al.* 2006). This 20-week intervention is delivered in groups of five to six caregivers, each session lasting 75 minutes. The first two weeks involves the use of an educational intervention to offer caregivers an explanation of attachment theory via video examples of their children expressing basic attachment and exploration needs. The next 18 weeks focus on individual caregivers with each caregiver being the focus of three sessions. During these sessions the therapist follows a manual protocol and uses edited video clips of the caregiver and child as a springboard to discuss the relationship and attachment patterns. This is aimed at helping the caregiver improve his or her capacity to read and respond to the child's cues and miscues regarding attachment exploration.

Box 6.4 Circle of Security

A young mother intrusively pursued her son as he sought a toy during play, which precipitated his pulling away as he attempted to explore; the son's refusal to play with the mother triggered her chilly withdrawal. On seeing this interaction in video review, and through reflective dialogue with the therapist, the mother recognized that she viewed her son's independent exploration as confirming her belief (negative attribution) that he does not want to be with her. In addition, she began to recognize that she typically manages the pain of his perceived rejection by withdrawing her support and creating distance. Further dialogue with the therapist led to her realization that her son needs her regardless of his activities and that when she supports his exploration he naturally comes back to her for connection when he is ready. (Hoffman *et al.* 2006, p.1021)

Population

The population comprised 65 toddler or preschooler–caregiver dyads recruited from Head Start and Early Head Start programmes. They were all at high risk of poor outcomes and many had experienced trauma or abuse during their childhoods. They ranged in age from 16 to 55 years and the mean age of the children was 32 months. Just under half were single, a third married and the remainder had a partner. Most (86%) were white Caucasian. A small minority of caregivers had at some point maltreated their children.

Child outcomes

The results show that 44 per cent of the pre-intervention insecure children shifted to a secure classification and that 69 per cent of the pre-intervention disorganized group moved to the organized group post-intervention. A small proportion of secure (8%) and organized (15%) children moved to insecure and disorganized categories post-intervention.

It is concluded that the Circle of Security protocol is a promising intervention for the reduction of disorganized and insecure attachment in high-risk toddlers.

Mentalization-based programmes

We identified one study (evidence level C) that had explored the effectiveness of mentalization-based therapy programmes for substance-abusing mothers (Suchman *et al.* 2008) and a case study (evidence level E) exploring the effectiveness of a similar therapy with a deprived mother and her baby (Slade *et al.* 2005). The studies were undertaken in Australia and the US respectively.

Mother and Toddler Programme

The Mother and Toddler Programme (MTP) comprises 12 weeks of individual therapy as an adjunct to standard outpatient substance-abuse treatment programmes. The programme is underpinned by psychosocial and neurobiological conceptual models with regard to attachment and addiction. The aim of the MTP is to improve maternal representational balance and capacity for reflective functioning and to increase maternal capacity for sensitivity and responsiveness to toddler emotional cues (Suchman *et al.* 2008, p.502). The early sessions focus on building a strong therapeutic alliance and to assist the mother to address whatever challenging circumstances she is facing at that time, including both concrete (e.g. financial problems) and relational issues. The next stage involves 'ensuring that the mother has adequate support and skills for tolerating and regulating strong affect (both positive and negative) because parenting stress can trigger strong and unregulated affective responses that, in turn, can precipitate a relapse to substance use' (p.503). Behavioral cues such as restlessness, hyperactivity, defensiveness, opposition, recurring crises or physical complaints are discussed in an effort to help the mother to recognize and contain (and eventually understand) the affect. The aim of this part of the therapy is 'clarification of the mother's representational world' in order to identify 'areas of distortion, harshness, incoherence, and insensitivity' that can be explored with a view to developing a more 'coherent and integrated understanding of herself and her toddler' (p.503). Attempts are made to link these representations with the way in which the mother is interacting with others, including her baby, the ultimate objective being to enable her to engage in a 'mentalizing process about the mother–child relationship'. The therapy also involves exploring what emotions are elicited when she focuses on her toddler playing, through the observation of videotaped play sessions.

Population
The intervention was delivered to eight outpatient substance-abusing women with toddlers aged 12 to 36 months. Sixty-four per cent were married or cohabiting. Seventy-one per cent were unemployed at the time of enrolment, 14 per cent not having completed high school. A majority were Caucasian, with 14 per cent Hispanic and 14 per cent African-American.

Parent outcomes (see Appendix 2 for detailed reporting)
The results show that mothers who completed the MTP had moderate improvements in representational balance and reflective function, which corresponded with significant improvements in their behaviours towards their toddlers. There were also significant improvements in drug use.

The authors conclude that this pilot study provides promising results to suggest that attachment-based interventions of this type can strengthen the capacity of substance-abusing mothers to support their child's socio-emotional development.

Minding the Baby programme
The following case study (evidence level E) explored the role of a mentalization-based therapy in the treatment of a mother and infant. It was conducted with a disadvantaged mother (ethnicity undefined) of an infant identified as being at high risk of abuse and neglect.

MENTALIZATION-BASED TREATMENT OF MOTHER AND INFANT
The 'Minding the Baby' programme is based in a community health centre that provides health care for people in poor and ethnically

diverse urban community. The programme was linked to health providers, but was administered by masters levels clinicians who were trained to assess and manage complex clinical issues in a highly disadvantaged and often traumatized population.

Mia, a 17 year old girl 7½ months pregnant who was taking part in a prenatal care group, was referred to a nurse and clinical social worker team at 'Minding the Baby'. Mia, who lived with her boyfriend Jay in his parents' chaotic and dirty house, was doing everything she could to disavow the reality of the baby and of her own internal world and referred to the infant as 'that' or 'my belly'. This unwanted pregnancy interfered with Mia's own desire, and her mother's hope, that Mia would get an education. Mia had a remarkable ability to verbalize her feelings of pain, anxiety and confusion about the child, something which was a valuable resource to the intervention team. The two practitioners began by helping Mia 'make room' for her child by creating a physical space for the baby and helping her envision and plan for an infant's physical needs.

Mia gave birth to a healthy girl but suffered from post-partum depression which peaked a month after birth. Mia rejected psychiatric treatment, and it was agreed that in addition to nursing visits, a social worker would visit her weekly. Mia cared for Noni physically but did not willingly touch her and left her alone for extended periods. At this point it was possible to start discussing Mia's past. Mia's mother had been a drug addict (as Mia's father had been) who had 'come clean' and who loved her daughter but who had also lost interest in her when she was five years old. Mia's mother's dreams for a better future for her daughter had been sabotaged by Mia's pregnancy.

Over the next few months, Mia forged a relationship with the social worker, in which she allowed herself to remember and describe moments and fears long forgotten, creating a narrative about her past that enabled her to better understand the present. The social worker validated Mia's care for the baby's physical, if not emotional, needs. Mia sometimes engaged in threatening behaviors, looming over the child, apparently delighting in the infant's grimace and frozen expression and asserting that the infant was 'faking' hunger cues. Workers did not address these deficits directly, but focused on helping Mia to understand the emotion that the baby's crying elicited and to trace a causal link between events in her past and her reaction to the child. As the intervention proceeded, Mia began to view the baby's intentions and affects with increasing accuracy and clarity, without needing to distort them in order to protect her fragile sense of self. Slowly, she became able to step outside her automatic reactions and observe her child's feelings. The baby began to express a more extended range of emotions to her now available mother. Although Mia continued her relationship with Jay, she decided to move back to her mother's cleaner, safer and child-friendly accommodation. The intervention was complemented by practical support, as workers brought toys to help Mia learn to play with the baby, and offered advice on vocational planning, medical care and training in safety procedures.

When Noni was 14 months old (17 months after Mia had entered the programme) the social worker reviewed a videotape made when the baby was 4 months old. Mia was troubled by her own lack of sensitivity, noting signs of distress that she was now able to identify. At 20 months, the baby was thriving, showed signs of secure attachment and was clearly loved by her mother, father (who still lived with his own family but was involved with his daughter) and her extended family.

(Slade *et al.* 2004, pp.85–91)

Combined approaches

We identified one Austrian study (evidence level C) that had evaluated a combination of approaches including interaction guidance, feeding training and individual therapy for families with infants diagnosed as non-organic failure to thrive (Dunitz *et al.* 1996), and one Israeli case study (evidence level E) of the implementation of a combined approach involving child–parent psychotherapy (CPP) and interaction guidance, in an outpatient psychiatric unit (Keren and Tyano 2001).

Combined interventions

The intervention evaluated in the Dunitz *et al.* (1996) study comprised a mixture of interaction guidance, clinic-based training in child feeding, and the parent's choice of therapeutic and counselling service.

Population

The study involved 76 parents (48 mothers and 28 fathers) of 50 first-born infants diagnosed with non-organic failure to thrive (FTT). Ninety-four per cent were white, and 6 per cent black. The age and socioeconomic status of the participating parents were not specified, but 42 per cent were single mothers and 2 per cent single fathers.

Outcomes for parents (see Appendix 2 for detailed reporting)

At baseline 38 per cent of parents were diagnosed as having an Axis I psychiatric disorder (e.g. depressive disorders, brief reactive psychosis, dysthymnia, somatoform disorders, reactive attachment disorder, alcohol dependence, impulse control, gender identity disorder and sedative dependent disorder) which was reduced to 37 per cent post-intervention, and 12 per cent at one-year follow-up. At baseline all of the parents were diagnosed (e.g. using ZTT-DC:

0-3 manual) as having relationship psychopathology (e.g. over-involvement, under-involvement, anxious-tense and mixed relationship diagnosis), and this was reduced to approximately 50 per cent at one-year follow-up.

Outcomes for children
The study found that all infants achieved normal physical growth within the time period of the intervention.

Case study of combined approach
We identified one further case study exploring the implementation of a combined approach (Keren and Tyano 2001) involving child–parent psychotherapy (CPP) and interaction guidance, in an outpatient psychiatric unit. This particular model of intervention involved an integration of modalities derived from attachment, trauma, cognitive-behavioural and social learning theories. Mother and child were seen in joint sessions (approximately once a week) and concurrent individual sessions were arranged with the mother when indicated. The intervention was conducted over approximately 50 weeks.

PSYCHOTHERAPY AND INTERACTION GUIDANCE FOR MOTHER AND INFANT

This case study involves 'S', a one-month-old first-born child of two young parents referred by the community health nurse because of concerns about mother's possible post-natal depression. At the first home visit, therapists observed the infant's feeding difficulties (although 'S' had not reached the FTT threshold) and noted the negative attributions of the mother ('A') of her baby's behaviour. A said, for example, that the infant 'is angry at me all the time, even when I feed her'.

A had a history of severe deprivation as the child of a drug-dependent mother, and had been sexually and emotionally abused. One particular traumatic loss appeared to influence A's feelings towards S. A had witnessed the death of her nine-year-old sister in an accident. A's loss was projected onto the child. She was filled with remorse at not having saved her sister's life, while at the same time believing that in some way, her sister had been reborn as S. The child's cries represented her (dead) sister's anger.

Therapists had three objectives: (i) to help A differentiate between her dead sister and the child; (ii) to provide developmental guidance; and (iii) to help create an emotional space for the child's true self, rather than the child imagined by her parent, by voicing the child's needs.

Two treatment modalities were combined: mother–infant psychodynamic therapy and interactional guidance, which is explicitly based on strengths (McDonough et al. 2000). Practitioners try to convey that parents are doing the best they can, address what parents see as the problem, answer questions posed by the family, provide information when asked and jointly with parents – define treatment goals and success.

The treatment stages focused on (i) provision of nurture for A, in order to help her become able to care for the child; (ii) enabling A to create a symbolic representation of the child. For example, the therapist sometimes spoke in lieu of the child, 'voicing' the child's feelings and desires; (iii) helping A to mourn her sister's death; when S's cognitive and motor skills developed, and it became clear to A that S was not her dead sister.

Therapy ended when S was 18 months old, but resumed after S developed selective mutism after starting school. At this point the father, who had resisted treatment, became involved, enabling some resolution of partner conflict. Dyadic therapy ended when the child was four, but both mother and child were referred to individual treatment.

(Keren and Tyano 2001, pp.57–60)

Strengths and limitations of the evidence about parent–child-focused treatments

Study designs

Three of the studies (Cicchetti *et al.* 2006; Toth *et al.* 2002, 2006) included in this section met the gold standard in terms of rigour, comparing two active treatments (e.g. parent–child psychotherapy and a cognitive-behavioural intervention) with a standard treatment control group. The remaining included studies were either controlled studies (i.e. no randomization) or one-group pre- and post designs (i.e. no comparison group) or case studies. Overall therefore, the evidence about parent–child focussed interventions is not robust and requires more rigorous evaluation.

Study interventions

The included studies adopted a range of innovative and interesting methods of working with parent–child dyads derived from a range of theoretical approaches including psychoanalytic and attachment theory.

Study populations

All of the included studies were directed at preschool or younger children, and only one of the included studies explicitly focused on parents diagnosed as emotionally abusive or at risk of being emotionally abusive. Two studies focused on parents with severe mental health problems, and the remaining studies focused on infants diagnosed as having faltering growth. These have been included because the literature suggests that severe mental illness can be associated with seriously suboptimal parenting, and as was suggested in Chapter 2, parental behaviour is considered by some to be an inadequate predictor of emotional abuse, and child outcomes are a better focus of interest, including physical syndromes, such as psychosocial short stature and failure-to-thrive (Kavanagh 1982 in Iwaniec 1997b, p.371). Faltering growth (non-organic failure to thrive) is one example where acts of omission specifically in terms of a child's emotional needs may lead to the child's failure to grow.

Study outcomes

As with the earlier chapter on the effectiveness of parent-focused interventions, one of the limitations of the evidence collated in this section about parent–child-focused interventions is the use of outcomes that are only indirect measures of emotional abuse. For example, the only study that included children diagnosed as emotionally abused, only assessed the impact of the intervention on proxy measures of emotional abuse (Toth *et al.* 2002). No assessment was made of objective measures of abuse. Furthermore, many of the studies evaluated outcomes that were directly related to the nature of the intervention. For example, one study evaluating the effectiveness of a representational form of parent–infant psychotherapy only assessed maternal and child representations (Toth *et al.* 2002); and one case study assessing mentalization-based parent–infant psychotherapy primarily focused on the development of the mother's ability to mentalize her infant (Slade *et al.* 2005). The only study that compared the effectiveness of two interventions (i.e. parent–infant psychotherapy with a cognitive-behavioural parenting programme) involved the use of outcomes that were likely to favour the parent–infant psychotherapy (Toth *et al.* 2002).

Summary

One of the strengths of the available evidence on the effectiveness of parent–child-focused interventions in preventing the recurrence of emotional abuse is the innovative nature of many of these methods of working. However, while the evidence about the effectiveness of some of these interventions with 'at risk' populations is now clearly established (e.g. see Bakermans-Kranenberg *et al.* 2003), rigorous evidence of their effectiveness with emotionally abusive populations is still seriously limited. Furthermore, the nature of some of these interventions means that they are limited in terms of their application to parents of infants and preschoolers.

7

Family-Focused Interventions

Introduction

This chapter examines the findings of our search to identify family-focused interventions (Figure 7.1) that are aimed at preventing the recurrence of emotional abuse. Such interventions seek to change maladaptive interactions between numerous family members, rather than the behaviour of one or more individuals in isolation from each other. Sessions may involve one or two members, parents and children, or even extended family members.

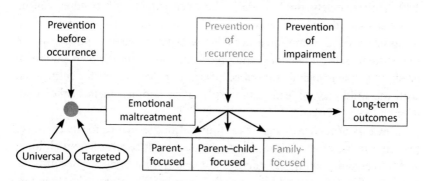

Figure 7.1 Focus of intervention

The chapter will address which family-focused interventions have been evaluated, which appear to work and who they work best with, and will conclude with an exploration of the strengths and limitations of the evidence.

What has been evaluated?

Family therapy

Family therapy seeks to change maladaptive interactions between family members. Sessions may involve one or two members, parents and children, or even extended family members. Although family therapy is an eclectic discipline, it draws substantially from Minuchin's (1974) work on family systems. Minuchin theorized that families have two principal subsystems – that of parents and that of their children. Clear, but permeable boundaries are required between the two in order to ensure the healthy functioning and communication of family members. Boundaries are blurred when children are used for instrumental purposes, in order to act as parents to adult caretakers who have profound unmet emotional needs, and when they are deployed as 'hostages' in conflict between adults (Cirillo and di Blasio 1998). While short-term caretaking responsibilities may be necessary and actually beneficial to children, 'destructive parentification, where children internalise ongoing expectations to care for parents' practical and emotional needs, has been associated with a range of emotional difficulties includ-ing depression, shame, anxiety and social isolation' (DiCaccavo 2006, p.469). Attention has also been drawn to the way in which a particular child becomes the scapegoat for conflict within the family. Children who are scapegoated may respond through externalizing behaviour (by becom-ing 'difficult to control') and drawing further attacks (Cirillo and di Blasio 1998). Alternatively, the boundaries between parents and children can be so rigid that adults are unavailable, cold and distant. Parents can fail to recognize a child's emotional boundaries 'when a parent's poor sense of self, extreme self-centeredness and preoccupation with their own emotional needs, which may include substance misuse, or a deep sense of identification with the child may all lead to the exploitation and detriment of the child' (Glaser 1995, p.76).

Reviews of family therapy have found strong evidence for its effective-ness in a range of conditions. These include conduct disorders in children and adolescents, eating disorders, substance misuse and as a second-line treatment for depression (Asen 2002). There is also an extensive literature on family therapy in cases of child sexual abuse and, to a lesser extent, parental violence (Carr 2006), and examples of short-term, intensive family therapy with families in which psychological maltreatment is recognized as compounding other forms of maltreatment (Fraser 1995). The aim of this review was to identify evidence about which family therapies work with emotionally abusive parents.

What works?

Systemic family therapy

In spite of the enormous importance of family systems theory in tracing the relationship between parental intra- or interpersonal conflict and phenomena such as 'scapegoating', fusion and/or parent–child role reversal, we identified only one case study (evidence level E) examining the role of family therapy in the treatment of emotionally abusive parenting (Byng-Hall 2002).

The following example illustrates the application of systemic, attachment-based family therapy to a case of parent–child role reversal (e.g. parentification) (Byng-Hall 2002).

SYSTEMIC FAMILY THERAPY AND PARENT–CHILD ROLE REVERSAL

Two-and-three-quarter-year Ann was referred for sleeping and eating disorders. She was the eldest daughter of middle-class parents (Margaret and Bruce) and sister of Susan, a 7-month-old baby. At bedtime, each parent took turns to try and get Ann to sleep, but when they left the room she would wake up and call for the other parent, and so on, late into the night.

Ann showed signs of parentification, the parents' relationship was conflicted and Margaret often threatened to leave Bruce. Ann appeared to take Margaret's threat at face value and call out at night to ensure that Margaret would stay. When the parents agreed to stop fighting in front of her, Ann's sleeping improved.

Therapy involved sessions with the parents and child, with Margaret and her own mother, and with Margaret and Bruce. The therapist invited Margaret's mother to two sessions. These helped Margaret recall her own experience of role reversal. Margaret's father had left when she was a child and Margaret was obliged to care for her own emotionally absent mother and grandparents. In therapy, Margaret began to recognise her own mother's inability to comfort her and Margaret's expectation that Ann would love her as her mother could not.

Bruce had been abandoned by his mother when he was ten, and like Ann (with whom he had forged a cross-generational coalition) he had expressed his anger at Margaret, who threatened to become like his mother and leave.

A central aim of therapy was to reduce the parents' need to turn to a child for care. In work with the couple, the therapist helped the couple to address their own conflicts without involving Ann, and to give and receive love and comfort from each other.

Ann's symptoms did not re-occur even when partner conflict re-surfaced, suggesting that she had been released from triangulation in her parents' relationship. After therapy ended, the couple was contacted yearly for seven years without further need for intervention.

(Byng-Hall 2002, pp. 382–387)

The authors observe that parentification is often ignored by therapists, and that while in certain situations (e.g. illness of a parent) children may, for a short time, be expected to take on additional responsibility ('constructive parentification') and that it is not necessarily harmful for short periods. Destructive parentification is, however, an expression of insecure attachment. It is suggested that therapists can utilize a range of approaches in order to promote secure attachment including: helping the family understand the strategies used in insecure family attachments that contribute to parentification; resolving parental conflicts and establishing appropriate generational boundaries; and working with parents so that they can understand the way in which transgenerational patterns have influenced their behaviours. A central aim in dealing with destructive parentification is to ensure that parents do not have to turn to children for care, by increasing support from other adults in order to avoid making demands on the child.

Family-based interventions
We also identified one UK case study (evidence level E) demonstrating the potential benefits of a range of interventions with different family members as well as the provision, in some cases, of practical support (Boulton and Hindle 2000). The study is based on the work of the authors at a child and adolescent psychiatric unit, which created a consultation group comprising at least one representative from four outpatient sector teams, one worker from the children's day unit (5–11 years) and one worker from the adolescent unit (a residential facility for young people 11–17). This case study draws attention to the flexibility required in working with families where children are emotionally abused.

The authors highlight a number of recurring features of many of the cases they encountered such as: re-enactment, unavailability and/or enmeshment (fusion). *Re-enactment* purports that at least one parent has suffered abuse or neglect in their family of origin and that as a result of these childhood experiences remaining undigested, unresolved or unavailable for thought, they are re-enacted in the relationship with the child. *Unavailability*, in which the parent is inaccessible to the child, and *enmeshment*, in which the boundaries between family members are diffuse, are also aspects of re-enactment. The following two case studies illustrate the way in which these features surfaced and were addressed.

CASE STUDY 1

Leah (9) is a second child. Her mother's first daughter was born with Down's Syndrome and an associated heart condition and had died aged 2½. Leah's mother's preoccupation with the sick child had meant there had been little opportunity to develop a relationship with her second daughter. She rarely spoke to or engaged with her. Leah's father remained fairly peripheral to the family and was unable to provide the emotional availability and containment Leah needed. Leah was referred to a child and adolescent psychiatry unit by her paediatrician because of concerns about Leah's aggression, soiling and concerns about mother's negative attitude towards her. On meeting the parents, the therapist recognised that they needed time to grieve the loss of their first child and to begin to reflect on their feelings towards Leah.

The therapist made herself available to the family for a long period, although she saw them infrequently. The focus of the therapy was to enable the parents to move from their complaints about the child to an understanding about her difficulties in establishing a place for herself in the family in the face of her sibling's illness and subsequent death. In time, the mother realised her need for help in her own right and sought referral to the adult mental health services. Her ability to 'own' the problems, rather than seeing them as being 'in' Leah, led to significant change.

(Boulton and Hindle 2000, p.446)

CASE STUDY 2

Elizabeth, aged 5, was considered difficult and triangulated in her parents' marriage. Elizabeth's mother's complaints were highly charged with emotion, words or deeds that might have been appropriate in the context of the parents' relationship with their own parent or caregiver. Elizabeth's mother had also been considered 'difficult' by her parents, and also, it transpired, triangulated in her parents' marriage (this could be also be described as a form of parentification).

The therapists worked with Elizabeth's mother and her maternal grandmother. This helped the grandmother take responsibility for family difficulties and relieve some of the guilt felt by Elizabeth's mother for her behaviour as a child. This, in turn, enabled Elizabeth's mother to stop treating Elizabeth as the 'container' for the more difficult parts of herself, take appropriate responsibility for the problems in her present family, and blame Elizabeth less for the struggles in her marriage.

(Boulton and Hindle 2000, p.448)

These cases illustrate the way in which the team worked with the 'past in the present'. It is suggested that the more information therapists were able to obtain about the family history of parents who had emotionally abused their children, the more easily they were able to formulate hypotheses about the effect of past events, and aid 'recognition' in which parents were able to begin to understand the effect of their history on their present behaviour. This approach is very similar to some of the psychotherapeutic interventions described in Chapters 5 and 6. The inclusion in this case of extended family members – particularly grandparents – was also found to be valuable.

It is also suggested that interventions are likely to require a long-term commitment, because parents tend to slip back to past maladaptive behaviours after a period of change, and the authors conclude that some families are likely to do this on a regular basis. Families with more complex problems were also provided with practical help (e.g. through a day centre for children), and it is suggested that this often proved most valuable in helping to sustain change.

The authors conclude that the identification, assessment and treatment of emotional abuse demands a multidisciplinary approach because of the complexity and multi-factorial nature of the task (Boulton and Hindle 2000, p.439), and that because of the asymptomatic condition of some children, the nature of problems may be difficult to discern.

Strengths and limitations of the evidence

Study design
We were unable to identify any rigorous evaluations of the effectiveness of family-focused interventions to prevent the recurrence of emotional abuse. We identified only two papers summarizing a number of case studies. This very probably reflects the fact that alternative terminology has been used to define family therapy papers.

Study interventions
The two included case studies provide examples of a number of ways of working with families in whom emotional abuse is an issue, including the application of an attachment-based systemic family therapy, and the use of a multidisciplinary professional network that provides therapeutic and practical support to all family members.

Study populations
The study populations all comprised families who had been referred for treatment by paediatric and/or child protection services due to emotional

abuse, and included cases involving parentification/role reversal; emotional neglect; and a child's missocialization as the consequence of parents' profound anxiety.

Study outcomes

The major limitation is that a range of outcomes are described from a clinical perspective but not formally evaluated. For example, the case study of the systemic family therapy reports on clinician perceptions regarding parent–child interactions (e.g. mothers seeking care from her child); parent–parent interactions (e.g. increased provision of mutual support); shifts in parent–child coalitions and detriangulation; child externalizing behaviours (sleeping and eating problems), but does not indicate how these were assessed.

Summary

While there is extensive evidence that irrespective of its orientation (e.g. behavioural, supportive or systemic) family therapy is an effective means of intervening to support a range of family-based problems (Stratton 2005), we were not able to identify any studies explicitly addressing the effectiveness of family therapy in preventing the recurrence of emotional maltreatment. Absence of evidence is not, of course, evidence of ineffectiveness, and the two included case studies provide interesting examples of the potential value of family therapy to parent–child role reversal and underlying insecure attachment.

There is also limited evidence available regarding the effects of multidisciplinary family-focused interventions, and again, further research is needed. The included case study suggests the potential benefits of a multidisciplinary consultation group in both the identification and treatment of families in which emotional abuse has occurred.

Section Four

Implications for Practice

8

What Works to Prevent Emotional Maltreatment?

Introduction

Emotional maltreatment, including both emotional abuse and neglect, underpins all other forms of abuse, but it also occurs on its own. Notwithstanding the variation in definitions of child emotional maltreatment currently in use, there appears to be considerable consensus about the type of parenting that is emotionally harmful to children, and extensive evidence about its harmful effects. The aim of this review was to collate evidence published since 1990 about what works in preventing its occurrence and recurrence. Despite extensive searching and contact with a wide range of experts in the field, we were only able to identify a small number of methods of working with this group of families that had been tested rigorously. Furthermore, the populations with whom these interventions had been evaluated were diverse (including drug-abusing parents, and children with non-organic failure to thrive/faltering growth). Despite these problems, we have identified a number of innovative ways of working with families for which there is at least preliminary evidence, or for which there is sometimes wider evidence of effectiveness with subtypes of abuse other than emotional maltreatment. This chapter will examine some of the key findings from our search for evidence and the final chapter will examine the key policy and practice implications.

What works in preventing the occurrence of emotional maltreatment

The profound impact of emotional abuse and neglect, particularly when it occurs during the very early years of life, suggests that intervention in infancy and toddlerhood may be critical if the negative consequences of emotional maltreatment are to be avoided (see O'Hagan 2006). Difficulties in the identification of emotional maltreatment (Boulton and Hindle 2000), alongside the absence of a consensus about how to distinguish it from suboptimal parenting (Trickett *et al.* 2009), and debate about the appropriateness of formal child protection processes for dealing with it (Glaser and Prior 1997), all point to the importance of intervening early to *prevent its occurrence.*

Prevention before occurrence (i.e. primary prevention) involves the use of population-based interventions that are aimed at promoting the type of early parenting that is now recognized to be necessary for optimal child development, alongside the use of targeted interventions that are often directed at improving parental sensitivity.

Population-based approaches

We identified no studies of the effectiveness of population-based approaches to the prevention of emotional maltreatment *before it occurs*, and this reflects a lack of evidence concerning population-based interventions more generally. However, as was argued in Chapter 3, a population-based approach to the primary prevention of emotional maltreatment is necessary because population surveys suggest a high prevalence (i.e. 6% for severe emotional abuse, and 30% for less severe forms of emotionally abusive parenting (Cawson *et al.* 2000). This points to the need to reduce the population pool of parents who may contribute to both potential and substantiated cases of emotional maltreatment. There is also a need to increase the use of de-stigmatizing access points to potentially useful approaches such as parenting programmes (e.g. mass media, primary health care services, schools and child care centres (Sanders 2008)).

There has been a significant increase in the number of parents exposed to materials and interventions such as leaflets, videos, television programmes and group-based parenting programmes, which have been shown to be effective in improving a number of psychosocial risk factors for emotional maltreatment, including parental mental health problems (Barlow *et al.* 2002) and child behaviour problems (Dretzke *et al.* 2009). While the overall population penetration is still insufficient to address the problem of emotional maltreatment, recent evidence suggests that higher levels of penetration can be achieved through the use of a population-based approach to their implementation, and that such strategies can impact on child abuse more generally. The study by Prinz *et al.* (2009) showed that the implementation of Triple P professional training to the child care workforce across health, social service and education settings in 18 US counties, alongside the use of universal media and communication strategies, was associated with a significant reduction in aggregate measures of child maltreatment including substantiated cases of child abuse. The implementation of this approach resulted in significant proportions of the child care workforce being able to deliver Triple P (e.g. education 25%; NGOs 24%; mental health and substance abuse services 19%; child care and preschools 16%; healthcare 10%; social services 4%).

Recent policy changes are also contributing to a change in practice. For example, the *Healthy Child Programme* which is part of the *National Service Framework for Children and Maternity Services* (Department of Health and Department for Education and Skills 2004) is underpinned by a model of progressive universalism (Department for Education and Skills 2007). As such, this nationally implemented health promotion and surveillance programme incorporates a range of universal and targeted strategies that can be used by primary care professionals to promote the type of parenting that is recognized to be important to the emotional health of the infant and toddler. This includes, for example, the recommendation that all *routine* contact between professionals and parents be used as an opportunity to promote sensitive and attuned parenting using a range of evidence-based approaches (including media-based strategies such as leaflets; books and videos; skin-to-skin care; use of infant carriers and infant massage, etc.), and to observe and identify parent–infant/toddler/child interaction that requires further input using targeted approaches.

Targeted approaches

Chapter 2 examined evidence showing a strong association between a range of factors, such as parental mental health problems, substance misuse, parental conflict, domestic violence and child maltreatment. These issues are particularly significant in terms of emotional maltreatment because they are strongly associated with suboptimal parental sensitivity and neglect, both of which are significant causes of emotional and psychological problems in early and later childhood. Maternal insensitivity is strongly associated with insecure attachment, and particularly severe manifestations of parental insensitivity, such as parental 'Fr-behaviour' (i.e. that is both frightened and frightening), are a significant predictor of disorganized attachment (see Chapter 2). Both insecure and disorganized attachment patterns have been shown to be significant predictors of socioemotional maladaptation (e.g. Sroufe 2005).

There is significantly more evidence available concerning the benefits of intervening early to improve maternal sensitivity, and we included a systematic review of over 70 'attachment-based' interventions that found significant improvements in maternal sensitivity and infant attachment security, particularly in terms of those programmes that were initiated after six months of age and that targeted this particular outcome (Bakermans-Kranenburg *et al.* 2003).

What works in preventing the recurrence of emotional maltreatment

We examined a number of interventions aimed at preventing the recurrence of emotional maltreatment, which we grouped according to the population targeted – parent-focused, parent–child-focused, and family-focused. Overall, there was a paucity of rigorous evaluations across all three categories, and it seems likely that one of the reasons for this is that the term 'emotional maltreatment' and some of its derivatives are still not being used systematically at the current time in relation to either the provision or evaluation of services and interventions that have secondary prevention and treatment-related aims and outcomes. We were, nevertheless, able to identify a number of approaches for which there is preliminary evidence of effectiveness, and the following sections summarize the key findings for each group of interventions.

Parent-focused interventions

The evidence about the effectiveness of parent-focused interventions to prevent the *recurrence* of emotional abuse is complex due to the wide-ranging interventions and populations with whom they have been evaluated. Although the characteristics that define parents who respond well to cognitive-behavioural therapy (CBT) approaches are not currently clear and the evidence appears to be limited to parents at the less severe end of the spectrum, the research nevertheless points to the potential value of providing CBT-based interventions to emotionally abusive parents. Furthermore, while there is only limited evidence currently available about the benefits of specific CBT-based interventions with emotionally abusive parents, some parenting programmes (e.g. Triple P) have been shown to be highly effective more generally across a wide range of outcomes, many of which are proxy measures of emotional abuse (e.g. parental anxiety and depression).

There is also evidence of the potential value of additional components that are specifically aimed at addressing factors known to be associated with emotionally abusive parenting (e.g. additional anger management and attributional retraining; stress and problem-solving training; and the use of mindfulness techniques aimed at improving negative parental affect). This points to the need for multi-level interventions or methods of working that target not only parenting practices but other factors that may be affecting the parent, including mental health problems, domestic violence, and substance misuse.

We were only able to identify two evaluations of the effectiveness of parenting interventions targeting parents with mental health problems, and families in which domestic violence is a problem. This is reflected in practice, where little attention is currently given to the potential for maltreatment where such problems are present, and points to the need for better partnership working between adult and children's services.

Substance abuse is also a major cause of child emotional maltreatment in terms of the missocialization of children (i.e. the process of witnessing such events), in addition to the other emotional and psychological consequences that occur to children who are exposed to environments characterized by parental insensitivity and emotional neglect. Most interventions that are currently available to support drug-abusing parents do not address the parenting issues that are associated with such drug use. Our search identified preliminary evidence of the effectiveness of a number of innovative ways of working with this group of parents including a developmentally informed, supportive psychotherapy group, and an intensive, ecologically based and multifaceted intervention (Parents under Pressure programme) targeting a number of domains of family functioning, in addition to the standard methadone support. Both interventions were explicitly aimed at reducing the risk of child maltreatment and improving parenting, *in addition* to addressing the primary problem of drug abuse. Further research is needed to address the problems identified by these early studies, such as the loss of effectiveness at six months in one study (possibly due to the abrupt withdrawal of the intervention), and to assess their effectiveness more widely in a range of UK settings.

Parent–child-focused interventions

Although we were once again unable to find many rigorous evaluations of parent–child-focused interventions specifically targeting emotional maltreatment, we nevertheless identified a number of highly innovative ways of working with parents and young children (i.e. preschool) including parent–infant/child psychotherapy, and video-interaction guidance. These dyadic methods of working involve the use of current interactions between the parent and child either to identify problems in the parents' representations, which are then addressed through the therapeutic process and relationship (representational parent–child psychotherapy) or to support more positive interactions (behavioural video-interaction guidance). Although these two approaches are underpinned by contrasting theoretical models, attempts to compare them to date have been limited. Other research suggests the value of utilizing both approaches together (e.g. Watch, Wait and Wonder – Cohen *et al.* 1999), or of applying the most appropriate method to meet the parent's needs based on the parent's internal working model (Bakermans-Kranenburg *et al.* 1998).

Other innovative ways of working, including a mentalization-based parenting programme underpinned by techniques drawn from both psychotherapeutic and home visiting interventions, are still very poorly supported by the evidence (we identified only two case studies). While this points to the need for further research, some of the new ways of working identified in this section have been shown to be effective in improving other outcomes that are strongly associated with emotional abuse, or to be effective in terms of other subtypes of child abuse. For example, there is currently a paucity of evidence available about the benefits of intensive home visiting programmes for emotionally abusive parents. However, the Family Nurse Partnership (FNP) programme has been shown to be effective in reducing child physical maltreatment (see Rowe 2009 for an overview), and is underpinned by a theoretical model which targets parent–child attachment and parental sensitivity. This suggests that such an approach is also likely to reduce emotional abuse, and future applications and evaluations of the FNP programme should include measures of emotionally abusive parenting as an outcome.

Family-focused interventions

Although family therapy is a widely evaluated intervention and has been shown to be an effective means of intervening to support a range of family-based problems (Stratton 2005), we were not able to identify any studies explicitly addressing its effectiveness in preventing the *recurrence* of emotional maltreatment. We also found an absence of evidence regarding the effects of multidisciplinary family-focused interventions. It seems likely that once again this reflects the terminology that is being used to describe both the application and evaluation of such interventions. For example, family therapy is currently offered within many mental health services to families where harmful patterns in relationships have resulted in the referral of a child for problems such as internalizing or externalizing problems, without this being defined as emotional maltreatment.

The case studies that we identified provided evidence of the successful application of family-focused approaches in the treatment of child emotional maltreatment, and also the potential benefits of a multidisciplinary consultation group in both the identification and treatment of families in which emotional maltreatment has been identified.

There is an urgent need for a rigorous evaluation of the effectiveness of family-focused interventions of this nature in the treatment of families in which emotional maltreatment is taking place.

Limitations of this review

Although we included a wide range of studies and search terms we will no doubt have missed studies that might have been eligible, had other definitions of emotional maltreatment been applied. Furthermore, as noted earlier, there is not only a need for more rigorous evaluation of interventions, but also for a more systematic application of the term emotional maltreatment in terms of the classification of studies in electronic databases.

Collation of evidence about the effectiveness of tertiary preventive interventions directed at children who have experienced emotional maltreatment was beyond the scope of this study and such a review is needed.

Concluding comments

Emotional maltreatment has very serious consequences in terms of the long-term development and wellbeing of children, and approaches to dealing with it should focus on the implementation of strategies needed both to prevent its occurrence, alongside strategies to prevent its recurrence.

Further research is urgently needed to evaluate the benefits of a number of different ways of working with emotionally abusive parents including cognitive-behavioural interventions, differing models of individual and group psychotherapy for parents and carers, and for parent–child dyads, and family therapy. Further research is also needed on the short- and long-term benefits of some of the more innovative methods of working that were identified, including parent–infant/child psychotherapy, video-interaction guidance, and other attachment and mentalization-based approaches. This is especially necessary in relation to parents at the more severe end of the spectrum, fathers, and older children. We also need further evidence about which subtypes of emotional maltreatment respond best to which treatments, and, indeed, whether parents with particular characteristics or problems are more likely to respond better to one form of therapy than another. The application of non-judgemental, emotional harm-related key words to studies of interventions provided outside child protection contexts may enhance the findings of future systematic reviews in this area.

Absence of evidence does not equate with evidence of absence of efficacy, and much uni-disciplinary to inter-agency work is undertaken with families whose children suffer emotionally because of the harmful behaviours of their parents or carers, whether intentional or otherwise. Practitioners and commissioners of services within which such complex work is undertaken should acknowledge the importance of research to practice, and try where possible to facilitate further routine evaluation of interventions and services.

9

Implications for Practitioners and Policy Makers

Introduction

Despite considerable changes to children's services during the past decade there is still a need for further clarity about the best ways to intervene to prevent or ameliorate emotional maltreatment. There is also a need for a shift away from traditional models of working to more evidence-based practice, particularly in terms of the everyday interventions of key groups of practitioners such as social workers and health visitors. Some of the issues raised in terms of the management of emotional maltreatment reflect broader issues currently being faced by children's services more generally, not least of which is the poor match between needs and services (Axford 2009).

The remainder of this chapter will examine the implications of the findings of this review of the literature on emotional maltreatment in the light of what is already known about effective methods of working with parents and families more generally, and of recent policy statements concerning the delivery of services to children following the death of Baby Peter (Lord Laming 2009). We have emphasized the need for more evidence-based practice including the use of:

1. an evidence-based aetiological model to underpin practice

2. an evidence-based approach to the assessment of need

3. the implementation of evidence-based interventions aimed at *bringing about change* with high-risk families.

These findings support the conceptual framework underpinning the government's guidance on assessing children with additional needs and children in need (Social Work Taskforce 2009; Department of Health 2000), and the challenge now is utilizing them in the provision of services at all levels.

Evidence-based conceptual models

Aetiological models of both child development and maltreatment emphasize the way in which a wide range of factors influence parental and family functioning (e.g. Belsky 1993; Cicchetti and Carlson 1995; Cicchetti and Rizley 1981). In Chapter 1 we presented an ecological-transactional model of child abuse which combines some of the insights from these earlier models. This suggests that:

> parents and children function across multiple ecological domains with short and long term potentiating and compensatory factors nested within each of these ecologies. At any given time the various ecological domains may interact catalytically, just as risk and protective factors may either ignite or buffer maltreatment at the various levels. (DiLillo, Perry and Fortier 2005, p.373)

Recent research has confirmed this model and suggests that children's adaptation is affected by the quality of relationships and interaction across a number of family domains. Cowan and Cowan (2008), for example, have highlighted five major domains of family life (Box 9.1).

Box 9.1 Five-domain family process model of the connections between risk factors and child outcomes

1. The quality of the mother–child and father–child relationships.

2. The quality of the relationship between the parents, including communication styles, conflict resolution, problem-solving and emotion regulation.

3. The patterns of both couple and parent–child relationships transmitted across the generations from grandparents to parents to children.

4. The level of adaptation of each family member, his or her self-perceptions, and indicators of mental health and psychological distress.

5. The balance between life stresses and social supports outside the immediate family.

(Cowan and Cowan 2008, p.7)

This model suggests that it is the 'quality of relationships and the process of interactions within families that are central to the wellbeing of children' with attachment insecurity playing a significant role in the intergenerational transmission of relationship problems across generations (Cowan and Cowan 2008, p.7), and factors beyond the family creating a range of sources of stress or support. They suggest that many interventions aimed at supporting children's development often only focus on one or at most two of the five family risk and protective domains at a time.

It was argued in Chapter 2 that families in which emotional maltreatment is an issue typically face multiple stresses including parental mental health problems, substance misuse and substantial domestic conflict or actual violence, alongside other life stresses such as poverty, unemployment, low education and a lack of social support. Consistent application of an ecological-transactional model is needed in terms of both assessment and intervention with families, and would enable practitioners to assess strengths alongside problems, and transient alongside enduring problems, across a range of levels of functioning. This would result in the application of interventions targeting *multiple domains of family life*, and focusing not only on the *quality of family relationships* but the broader *life stressors* that many emotionally maltreating families typically face (Cowan and Cowan 2008).

An evidence-based approach to assessing need

Despite the fact that the number of children registered for emotional abuse has increased over the past ten years, much primary emotional maltreatment goes undetected. Emotional maltreatment that occurs during the first two years of life, when its impact can be most severe (due to its effect on the infant's developing brain, their attachment security, and their subsequent ability for emotional and behavioural regulation), is the least likely of all to be recognized, suggesting that its identification continues to pose problems for practitioners.

A number of texts describe some of the key processes and methods involved in a comprehensive assessment of whether a child is being emotionally maltreated (see, for example, O'Hagan 2006; Iwaniec 1997a), but what have we learned about the identification of child abuse more generally in the past decade? A recent review of the evidence on this topic found significantly higher rates of abuse than had been recognized to date (in the region of 10%), and that few maltreated children come to the attention of child protection agencies, indicating a failure of professionals to recognize it; a failure to report; and a failure to investigate or substantiate it (Gilbert *et al.* 2009). In terms of methods of working in child protection, a recent international study found that Nordic countries that adopt a *holistic* model of working (i.e. characterized by early intervention and preventive work based on a continuum of care; a strong family support focus; and a focus on 'failures of upbringing' and of harm to the child's social and emotional development) are more effective compared with the *dualistic* model that has until fairly recently been characteristic of English-speaking countries (i.e. dominated by the need to prevent abuse with family support provided separately) (Katz and Hetherington 2006).

In Chapter 1 we highlighted an important shift in UK government policy away from this dualistic model and towards a more holistic one, but we also highlighted research suggesting that professionals such as social workers may currently be straddling a rather uncomfortable divide in which 'guidance driven at a national level by research and policy is being worked out in an organisational context where local authorities continue to seek to manage child protection risks as their first priority' (Spratt 2001). This research also suggested that there is still a very high threshold for access to services, with child protection being the surest way to receive an intervention (Spratt 2001).

The shift to a family support/welfare model of working, in addition to the need to focus resources strategically, means that practitioners need to begin focusing attention on assessing family need in terms of support, and whether the change that is achieved as the result of such support is sufficient to ameliorate the most significant risks to the child's development. Recent criticism of the assessment process has focused on its failure to meet minimal guidelines of best practice (Conley 2003 in Harnett 2007); the reliance on single rather than multiple sources of background information and the application of single domains of family functioning (child or parental) with no evaluation of broader ecological influences; and an absence of direct observations of parent–child interaction (Harnett 2007).

It has also recently been suggested that 'cross-sectional assessment of families provides important information about family functioning at one point in time, but is of limited usefulness when the results are equivocal' (Harnett and Dawe 2008, p.227), and that what is actually needed at such times is an assessment of a family's *capacity to change*, including an evaluation of the parent's motivation and capacity to acquire parenting skills. Harnett and Dawe (2008), whose evaluation of the Parents under Pressure (PUP) programme was explored in Chapter 5, suggest that this should include a number of steps (Box 9.2).

Overall, these findings suggest the need for more evidence-based practice (EBP) in relation to the assessment of families in need, and the application of EBP to an assessment of the risk of harm is demonstrated in Figure 9.1.

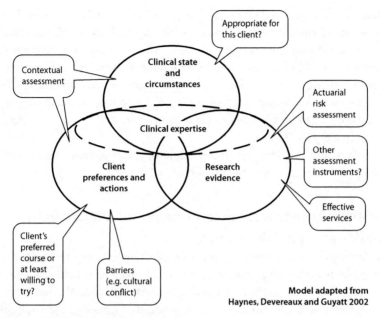

Figure 9.1 Evidence-based assessment

Box 9.2 Procedure for assessing parents' capacity for change in child protection cases

1. A cross-section assessment of the parents' current functioning including the use of a range of standardised psychological tests to supplement other sources of information and to include an assessment of parent–child interactions.

2. Specification of operationally defined targets for change that should include the unique problems facing individual families and using standardised procedures such as Goal Attainment Scaling – GAS.

3. Implementation of an intervention with proven efficacy for the client group that addresses multiple domains of family functioning, is delivered in the home, using individualised goals, and tailored to address the specific problems of individual families, and the achievement of identified targets for change.

4. Objective measurement of progress over time including standardised tests administered pre and post the intervention; direct observation of changes in parent–child interaction; and evaluation of the parents' willingness to engage and cooperate with the intervention and the extent to which targets were achieved.

(Harnett 2007, p.1179)

Shlonsky and Wagner (2005) suggest that evidence-based assessment should involve using current best evidence to identify and use reliable and valid tools to assess different aspects of a parent's functioning and environment, alongside their clinical expertise to undertake a contextual assessment to elicit key strengths and needs. Practitioners should then use current best evidence to make decisions about the most appropriate services to put in place alongside information about client preferences and potential barriers to success (see Figure 9.1).

This model provides just one example of the application of evidence-based practice to the assessment process.

Evidence-based working to bring about change with families at high risk of abuse

The findings of this review suggest that effective working to bring about change in (emotionally) abusive families will require further changes at both organizational/institutional and practitioner levels. We have argued throughout this book that the issue of emotional maltreatment, and child abuse more generally, requires the implementation of *both* primary preventive population-based and targeted interventions directed at stopping its *occurrence*, alongside secondary preventive interventions aimed at stopping its *recurrence*. The findings of this review suggest that what is needed to address the issue of emotional maltreatment is more evidence-based working with the explicit aim of bringing about change across a range of family domains.

It has recently been argued that 'children's services will produce measurable improvements in public health only when science-based prevention practices are institutionalised on a large scale' (Hill *et al.* 2008). However, it is also acknowledged that there are currently significant barriers to its institutionalization, including a false dichotomy between prevention (i.e. 'deficit') and promotional (i.e. 'strengths') approaches, and the 'inflexibility and cost of implementing packaged, evidence-based programmes' (Hill *et al.* 2008, p.41). There is also the need for further budget and resources to be dedicated to the implementation of high quality programmes. Hill *et al.* (2008) go on to argue that a number of flexible solutions are emerging to facilitate the adoption of science-based practices including evidence-informed programme improvement (EIPI) (Small, Cooney and O'Connor 2009). One such solution involves the use of systematic and flexible approaches to the implementation of evidence-based practices in programme planning, delivery and organization (see Box 9.3). Another involves the systematic incorporation of 'kernals' (i.e. brief, evidence-based interventions) into children's services and activities (Embry and Biglan 2008 in Hill *et al.* 2008).

Box 9.3 Principles of effective programmes

Programme design and content

- theory driven
- of sufficient dosage and intensity
- comprehensive
- actively engaging.

Programme relevance

- developmentally appropriate
- appropriately timed
- socioculturally relevant.

Programme implementation

- delivered by well-qualified, trained and supported staff
- focused on fostering good relationships.

Programme assessment and quality assurance

- well documented
- committed to evaluation and refinement.

(adapted from Small, Cooney and O'Connor in Hill *et al.* 2008, p.40)

We have argued here that where parenting has been defined as (emotionally) abusive, change is required across a number of family domains, and in Chapters 5 to 7, we examined some of the key theoretical models underpinning interventions that have been developed to prevent its recurrence, alongside the available evidence about which of them work. The principles of effective programmes have been clearly delineated (Box. 9.3), and what is now required to enable practitioners to work more effectively with families in whom (emotionally) abusive parenting practices are an issue is:

1. evidence-based core practice that enables practitioners to work *in partnership* with parents alongside an understanding of the processes involved in helping (Davis, Day and Bidmead 2002)

2. the application of evidence-based developmentally informed models

3. the implementation of interventions that meet the principles of effective programmes, not least of which is a clear programme theory specifying the mechanisms through which change will occur.

This requires 'a systematic approach to programme planning and development and consistent evaluation practices' (Hill *et al.* 2008, p.41), and there are now a number of tools to enable service providers to do this more effectively (see for example the Programming Planning and Evaluation toolkit (What Works, Wisconsin 2007). The remainder of this section examines each of the above criteria in turn.

1. Evidence-based core practice – working in partnership
It was suggested in Chapter 1 that research conducted since the 'refocusing initiative' showed that greater attention had been given to participatory or partnership practice and that this was favourable to families as a result of the implementation of the *Framework for the Assessment of Children in Need and their Families* (Cleaver and Walker 2004; Corby 2002), and that 'child welfare' cases lead to more 'successful relationships' (Spratt and Callan 2004). These findings are consistent with wider research which suggests that 'partnership working' is essential to enabling families to achieve change (Davis 2009).

As with other evidence-based interventions, most models of partnership working are underpinned by empirically validated concepts with regard to the process of change, and require that practitioners are trained in its principles and implementation, and receive ongoing support. This is exemplified, for example, by the Family Partnership Model (see Figure 9.2), which teaches practitioners the *core* components of the helping relationship.

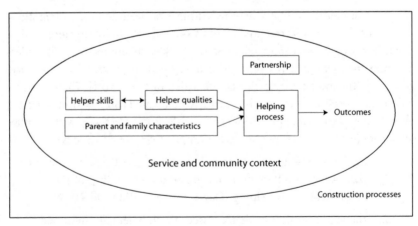

Figure 9.2 The Family Partnership Model

Box 9.4 Construing

- People constantly take in and process information so as to make sense of their world.
- They construct a model of the world in their heads.
- This enables them to anticipate and adapt to whatever happens to them.
- This model is derived from their past experiences.
- Each person has a unique set of constructions, which are not necessarily conscious or easily verbalized.
- These constructions are constantly being tested, clarified and changed.
- Social interaction is determinded by our contrustions of each other.

The Family Partnership Model is an evidence-based model of partnership working, based on the 'constructionist' work of Kelly (1991), which defines 'how people function psychologically and socially', and suggests that 'both parents and helpers develop a unique understanding of their world in order to anticipate and adapt to events' (Davis *et al.* 2002, p.70). A major implication of this is that the process of facilitating change involves 'challenging parental constructions', to enable people to develop more useful or effective 'constructions' (Davis *et al.* 2002, pp.70–1) (see Figure 9.2). For a full description of the model, see Davis, Day and Bidmead (2002).

Davis *et al.* (2002, p.68) suggest that 'since the task of building a relationship between the helper and the parent is crucial to the facilitation of the whole process and hence the outcomes, the nature of the relationship to which health professionals should work, must be carefully defined and represented as a specific ingredient within the overall model'. Perhaps most importantly, it is suggested that effective partnership working is characterized by the following factors:

- Working closely together with active participation and involvement.
- Sharing decision-making power.
- Recognition of complementary expertise and roles.
- Sharing and agreeing aims and process of helping.
- Negotiation of disagreement.

- Mutual trust and respect.
- Openness and honesty.
- Clear communication.

The Family Partnership Model defines the core tasks of the helping process (see Figure 9.3), and also specifies:

> the interpersonal skills needed to engage parents and facilitate the process (e.g. attentive and active listening, prompting them to talk and explore, responding empathically and negotiating), alongside the underlying, internal qualities of effective helpers (e.g. respect, genuineness, empathy, humility, quiet enthusiasm, personal integrity, attunement and technical knowledge, including an understanding of the processes of helping). (Davis *et al.* 2002, p.69–70)

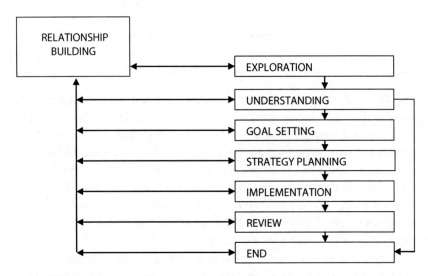

Figure 9.3 The process of helping: tasks

This suggests that the overall context for the partnership model consists of the services and community within which the helping process is conducted and includes the 'characteristics of the service, the population and the geographical area, but of particular importance for effective practice is the management and supervisory support available for service personnel. Within the Family Partnership framework it is assumed that the processes of such support are exactly parallel to the processes of helping and that the Model as outlined here applies to both' (Davis *et al.* 2002, p.70).

We suggest that key groups of practitioners, such as social workers and health visitors, should be selected on the basis of such interpersonal skills, and trained in the use of an evidence-based model of partnership working, such as the Family Partnership Model.

2. Implementation of evidence-based models of child development

The evidence strongly points to the need for an evidence-based child developmental model to underpin practice. The findings support the government's guidance in the *Framework for the Assessment of Children in Need and their Families* (Department of Health 2000) and the *Common Assessment Framework* (Social Work Taskforce 2009). In Chapters 5 to 7 we examined evidence underpinned by a range of aetiological models with regard to child maltreatment. The results of this review suggest that in order to work effectively with families, it is necessary that all practitioners have a clear understanding of the most significant developmental issues in terms of the impact on children of diverse aspects of the environment. Despite recent concern about its use to view all anomalies in social relationships (Rutter, Kreppner and Sonuga-Barke 2009), attachment theory is possibly one of the most widely researched concepts in the field. Recent developments in terms of the concept of 'disorganized attachment' are proving particularly useful in understanding the development of children who have experienced adverse early environments, including abuse or neglect. Attachment theory may also be one of the best evidence-based explanations that we currently have with regard to the intergenerational transmission of relationship patterns, and their associated problems (van IJzendoorn and Bakermans-Kranenburg 1997).

The use of an attachment-based developmental model would provide an evidence-based approach to conceptualizing the impact of the early environment on children, in terms of both identifying and intervening with children who have been emotionally abused. The application of such a model would involve:

- assessing the impact of the abuse in terms of the child's attachment system (i.e. their capacity to develop trusting relationships)

- intervening to address the child's attachment needs in terms of the support that is put in place to address problems at the level of both the parent and the child.

Most services and interventions being used with maltreating families address issues related to parental welfare and adaptation, and other aspects of the family's developmental ecology. We are arguing for a shift in emphasis to focus on the sensitivity and responsiveness of parental behaviour in the context of their interaction with the child, and an assessment of the benefits of intervention in terms of the improvement in the relationship with the parent and, thereby, the child's attachment system.

This would require that key groups of practitioners have the skills to:

- identify the impact of parenting on children's attachment, particularly in terms of their ability to recognize children showing signs of disorganized attachment

- work in partnership/therapeutically with families to bring about change.

The latter requires practitioners to develop some of the new ways of working (e.g. video-interaction guidance) that are now being disseminated, and for service commissioners to ensure the availability of other therapeutic methods of working for which there is now evidence of effectiveness (e.g. CBT-based parenting programmes; parent–infant/child psychotherapy).

3. Implementation of interventions that meet the principles of effective programmes

The principles of effective working are now well recognized and the next section of this chapter examines two contrasting interventions that have been examined as part of this review in terms of their programme design and content; relevance, implementation and assessment/quality assurance (see Box 9.4). We have selected these from a number of possible programmes, because they exemplify two contrasting approaches to the treatment of emotional abuse (i.e. cognitive-behavioural and psychotherapeutic) that nevertheless meet many of the above principles of effective programmes.

Triple P-Positive Parenting Programme

In terms of programme design and content Triple P comprises a number of factors that are recognized to be important to effective working. Perhaps the most important is that it is underpinned by a clear conceptualization of the processes that have contributed to the problem; the change that is needed to reduce the problem; and the method by which such change can be realized. The Triple P Programme is underpinned by a clear model of change with regard to improving parenting (see Box 9.5). For example, the literature on child abuse suggests that a key factor in its aetiology is a deficit in child management skills resulting in the use of coercive and punitive parenting strategies. This points to the value of implementing behavioural interventions (e.g. parenting programmes and behavioural family interventions) based on social learning principles, which have been widely shown to be effective in improving such parenting practices. The standard family intervention requires parents to attend four group sessions of parent-training (two hours duration each) followed by four individual telephone consultations (15–30 minutes duration each), and they also receive a copy of *Every Parents Group Workbook* (Markie-Dadds, Turner and Sanders; Sanders *et al.* 2004). They are taught 17 core child-management strategies designed to promote children's competence and development, and help parents manage misbehaviour. Parents are also taught a planned activities routine to enhance the generalization and maintenance of parenting skills. The training involves the use of a range of methods including modelling, rehearsal, practice, feedback and goal setting within a self-regulatory framework (Sanders 1999), aimed at helping parents to 'set and monitor goals for behaviour change and to enhance their skills in observing their child's and their own behaviour' (Sanders *et al.* 2004, p.523).

Box 9.5 Theoretical principles underpinning Triple P-Positive Parenting Programme

- Social learning models of parent–child interaction.
- Child and family behaviour therapy research.
- Developmental research on parenting in everyday contexts and social competence.
- Social information processing models.
- Developmental psychopathology research.
- Public/population health framework.

The research also suggests that 'maltreating parents tend to hold distorted beliefs and unrealistic expectations regarding the developmental capabilities of children, the age-appropriateness of child behaviours, and their own behaviour when interacting with children (Black *et al.* 2001). These cognitive distortions have been linked to parents attributing hostile intent to their child's behaviour, which in turn has been linked with over-reactive and coercive parenting (Bugental 2000); angry feelings in parents (Slep and O'Leary 1998); child behaviour problems (ibid); and the use of harsh punishment (Azar 1997)' (Sanders *et al.* 2004, p.515). The enhanced version of the Triple P Programme thus comprises an additional four sessions that are aimed explicitly at addressing cognitive (attributional retraining) and affective factors (anger management) that have been shown to differentiate between maltreating and other parents (Stern and Azar 1998 in Sanders *et al.* 2004). In these additional sessions, parents are taught 'a variety of skills aiming to challenge the beliefs they hold regarding their own behaviour and the behaviour of their child, and to change any negative practices they currently use in line with these beliefs' (Sanders *et al.* 2004, p.523). Parents are also taught 'a variety of physical, cognitive, and planning strategies to manage their anger' including the use of advanced planning for high-risk situations (p.523).

In terms of its relevance, Triple P comprises a number of programme variants that have been specially designed to address the needs of different groups of parents (e.g. Workplace Triple P; Pathways Triple P; Stepping Stones Triple P; Infant Triple P; Lifestyle Triple P, etc.) (see Figure 9.4).

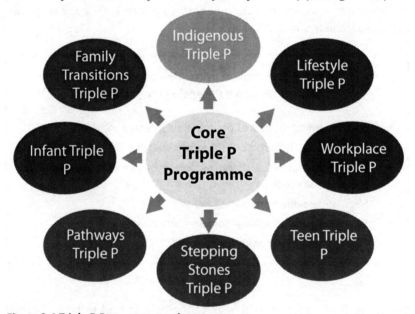

Figure 9.4 Triple P Programme variants

In terms of its implementation, as with many effective evidence-based interventions, Triple P comprises a manualized programme that is provided by fully trained practitioners, who receive ongoing support and supervision during its delivery. It also shows significant commitment to programme assessment and quality assurance with over 90 evaluations testifying to its effectiveness in a range of settings.

Parent–infant/child psychotherapy

We also identified some evidence of effectiveness of parent–infant/child psychotherapy with emotionally maltreating parents. As with CBT, a wider body of evidence is beginning to accumulate demonstrating the effectiveness of this form of psychotherapy with maltreated children (Toth and Cicchetti 1993 in Toth *et al.* 2002). As with the above intervention it is underpinned by evidence about the benefits of providing social support and the promotion of positive parenting, but also builds on an additional body of developmental research that conceptualizes the mother–child attachment relationship as central to positive child outcomes (Fraiberg, Adelson and Shapiro 1975; Lieberman 1991 in Toth *et al.* 2002). This literature suggests that 'in accord with attachment theory, it is through early experiences with care-givers that children are thought to develop complex mental structures, typically referred to as representational models, schemata, or internal working models' (Toth *et al.* 2002, p.879). A broad body of research shows that children who experience abusive or neglectful caregiving develop negative representations of caregivers and themselves, which are eventually generalized more widely to other relationships (Lynch and Cicchetti 1991 in Toth *et al.* 2002), and result in a range of deleterious outcomes including disorganized attachment (van IJzendoorn, Schuengel and Bakermans-Kranenburg *et al.* 1999 in Toth *et al.* 2002). This model posits that abusive parents have problems in terms of their interactional history and its effect on representation of relationships. The model aims to link current parental perceptions and responses to the child with the parent's earlier life experiences, particularly his or her own history of being parented, which are typically highly disturbed and often abusive.

Parent–infant child psychotherapy typically consists of 60-minute dyadic sessions with a clinical therapist involving joint observation of parent (usually the mother and child, allowing therapists 'to gain insights into the influences of maternal representation on parenting as maternal representations and distortions are enacted within the context of preschooler–parent interactions' (Toth *et al.* 2002, p.891). The intervention is designed to provide the mother with a 'corrective emotional experience' aimed at helping maltreating mothers to 'overcome these negative expectations and provide a holding environment for the mother and preschooler in which new experiences of self in relationship to others and to the preschooler may be internalised' (p.891). The therapist thus 'responds to maternal statements and interventional patterns, linking current maternal conceptualisations of relationships to mothers' childhood caregiving experiences' (p.891).

In terms of programme relevance, while this form of therapy is determined by the age of the child (i.e. it can only be used with infants and preschool children), recent variations have begun to emerge that build on findings from other theoretical models (e.g. Watch, Wait and Wonder combines psychotherapeutic with behavioural approaches). These variations also reflect the findings from recent evidence suggesting that therapy may be differentially effective for parents with different types of attachment insecurity (Bakermans-Kranenburg *et al.* 1998).

This form of therapy excels in terms of programme implementation because practitioner training is long, regular supervision is core to its delivery, and the fostering of good relationships is also central. In terms of assessment, there is a growing body of evidence pointing to the effectiveness of parent–infant psychotherapy (Cohen *et al.* 2000), and attachment-based interventions more generally (Bakermans-Kranenburg *et al.* 2003).

Putting children back at the heart of children's services

Article 12 of the 1989 UN Convention on the Rights of the Child recognizes the right of all children to have their views heard and responded to in matters that concern them, and this has been enshrined more recently in the Minimum Standards for Consulting with Children (Inter-Agency Working Group on Children's Participation 2007). Child-centred practice as encapsulated in the Children Act 1989 involves working with children in a way that *enables them* to express their wishes and feelings during assessment and for these to be taken into account in the decision-making process. This is in contrast with practice in which adults are presumed to be able to speak on behalf of their children.

The need to place the child at the centre of everything that practitioners do was highlighted again by Lord Laming's Progress Report (2009), and this was translated in the government's response as 'understanding the perspective of the child, listening to the child, and never losing sight of the child'. It goes on to state that 'Just as the centrality of the child drives our policies so too should it drive day-to-day practice at the front line' (Department for Children, Schools and Families 2009, p.4). This review confirms existing government guidance that points to the need to put the assessment of parent–child interaction at the heart of the family assessment process. Listening to and consulting with children should not be limited to attempts to enable them to express their concerns verbally or through play and, indeed, may not be possible, particularly where the child is of preschool age, or even pre-verbal. Thus, in addition to consulting verbally with children, one of the best ways of enabling them to express the difficulties that they are experiencing with the parenting that they are receiving, is for skilled and appropriately trained practitioners to undertake an assessment of the child in *interaction with the parent*. Such an assessment would enable practitioners to identify the emotional distress of infants, toddlers and young children who are not able to express this verbally, and also to identify problems that older children may not, for a range of reasons, be able to put into words.

One of the key issues highlighted in Lord Laming's recent Progress Report (2009) was the need to gather best practice in referral and assessment systems for children whose caregivers' ability to care for them is seriously compromised by domestic violence, mental health problems or alcohol and drug abuse. A failure to consult with children often translates into a failure to see the child at all. Possibly one of the key problems at the current time is the failure to recognize that children living in families that are experiencing this type of problem are *at substantially increased risk* of emotional maltreatment, as a result of the fact that parents experiencing such difficulties are often not in a position to meet the emotional needs of their children. All children living in families experiencing such problems should be given the opportunity to express the impact that this is having on them, and to receive support (Department of Health 2000). This should, once again, involve the *routine assessment of parent–child interaction* to gain an understanding of the problems, and the implementation of interventions or services that are aimed at enabling the parent to function better in their role as a parent and reducing the exposure of the child to parental distress and malfunctioning.

What package of services is required?

Two questions frequently posed by service commissioners and practitioners are which evidence-based programme should they be using and how is it possible to maintain the fidelity of such interventions given the unique needs of service users. The answer to the first part of the question is not easy because few studies actually compare the effectiveness of different services, making it difficult to know whether one model is superior to another. Furthermore, the evidence that has been examined in this review suggests the need for multimodal programmes that minimally assess the 'multiple influences across ecological domains' that are affecting a parent's ability to parent (Harnett and Dawe 2008). For example, it has been argued that decisions about what services to put in place should reflect an understanding that is well supported by the evidence that 'an intervention aimed at developing a parent's repertoire of parenting skills will have a greater impact on family functioning if the intervention also provides parents with skills to regulate their emotional state, deal more effectively with competing demands, and engage social support (see Gershoff 2002)' (Harnett and Dawe 2008, pp.2–3). Recent evidence suggests that even the use of intensive evidence-based programmes (such as, for example, the Parents under Pressure programme – see Chapter 5) may require additional ongoing support to enable parents both to reach a minimal level of adequate parenting, and to maintain it (Harnett and Dawe 2008). It has also been suggested that decisions about ongoing packages of care should be influenced not only by the profile of presenting problems but also by the patterns of change that have been observed across the key domains of functioning – parental psychological functioning; parenting skills; parent–child relationship; family functioning; and social context – in response to the implementation of a procedure to assess change (Harnett and Dawe 2008).

This suggests that key practitioners working in partnership with parents should have available to them a wide range of specialist and non-specialist services that can address the multiple unique needs of a family. While there is increasing availability of interventions such as parenting programmes, there is often little programme variation to meet the needs of different populations, and specialist services are rare or non-existent. We were not able to identify any evaluations of the effectiveness of parenting interventions for parents who are experiencing domestic violence, and a limited amount of evidence with regard to parents experiencing mental health problems.

While the issue of programme fidelity has been recognized to be core to effective implementation, many practitioners want the flexibility to adapt programmes to meet the needs of local participants. Programme implementation is often of poor quality (Bumbarger and Perkins 2008 in Axford *et al.* 2009) and recent research shows 'a clear, significant relationship between implementation quality and outcomes' (Durlak and DuPre 2008 in Axford *et al.* 2009, p.49). It has been suggested that the failure to implement a programme well can be the equivalent of doing nothing (Axford *et al.* 2009), and there is increasing recognition, therefore, of the value of *informed adaptation*, which it is suggested 'permits flexibility in areas of programme delivery not hypothesised to be directly responsible for programme outcomes but which do not detract from the Programme's theory of change' (Greenberg *et al.* 2005 in Axford *et al.* 2009, p.50). This could include, for example, making changes to programmes to ensure that they are culturally sensitive.

Conclusion

Emotional maltreatment of children is a significant problem in modern societies such as the UK, and is associated with a range of poor outcomes in childhood, adolescence and adulthood. Children are at increased risk of emotional abuse where one parent, particularly if this is the main carer, is experiencing mental health problems and drug or alcohol abuse, and in families where domestic violence is taking place. An assessment of the impact of these problems on child wellbeing should be routine.

The identification of emotional maltreatment requires an assessment of parent–infant/child interaction as part of a broader assessment of family functioning such as the assessment of children in need (Department of Health 2000). This should be undertaken by practitioners who have received training in observing and classifying parent–child interactions using standardized and validated tools, as part of a broader assessment of the family. An assessment of parent–child interaction should be a significant part of the evaluation of any family in which child abuse is suspected, but is particularly important in the case of emotional maltreatment, which consists of repeated patterns of harmful interactions between parent and child, rather than specific events. Such assessments would enable practitioners to identify harmful interactions that are unlikely to be detected without the use of such tools. We have argued for the need for an assessment of the impact of parenting on the child's attachment system and for these to be central to assessing what needs to be done.

These findings support the need for both organizations and practitioners to be working with families to *bring about change* and the need for practitioners to have core evidence-based partnership working skills. They also support the implementation of an evidence-based family assessment process that has at its heart an assessment of the parent–child relationship, and the potential impact of this relationship on a child's development and wellbeing, including their capacity for attachment relationships. This should be followed by the implementation of evidence-based intervention(s), targeting key domains of family functioning and interaction.

There is a need for further financial resources that are focused explicitly on evidence-based programme planning, delivery and organization alongside a need for changes to the core training of key groups of practitioners including social workers and health visitors, and continuing professional development. This should be aimed at up-skilling these key groups of practitioners to enable them to acquire some of the evidence-based methods of working that have emerged over the past decade.

It has been suggested that there is a need for a national transformation to children's services that involves 'new training, new programmes and a focus on the details of implementation with more coherent and consistent planning by local authorities' (Axford 2009, p.47). This review supports such a suggestion, and the final section of this chapter examines some of the key recommendations of this review.

Key findings
Terminology and conceptual issues

- New terminology is needed to refer to the wide range of emotionally abusive parenting practices that are now recognized as being damaging to children. For example, *emotionally harmful interactions* could be used to describe a wide range of suboptimal parenting practices that are harmful to the child and for which family support is required; and *harmful family environment* could be used to characterize families that may be experiencing a wide range of problems that are likely to have considerably adverse effects in terms of children's development.

- Practice should be underpinned by an ecological-transactional model in terms of both assessment and intervention with (emotionally) abusive families to ensure the targeting of diverse and significant factors affecting the families' functioning.

Training and support

- The preparation of core groups of practitioners (e.g. social workers and health visitors) should include training in evidence-based practices to enable them to establish participatory and partnership working with families alongside an understanding of the key factors involved in the helping process.
- The training of core groups of practitioners should include preparation to enable them to:
  - use evidence-based assessment, which should include training to enable them to use standardized methods to assess parent–child interaction using validated tools
  - implement evidence-based practices/interventions with families.
- Emotionally harmful interactions on the part of parents appear to be common. Considerable benefit could be realized through the implementation of both *population* and *targeted* approaches aimed at *preventing the occurrence of such interactions* in both population and high-risk families.
- Assessment of harmful parent–infant/child interaction using standardized and validated tools could be used to target resources more effectively.
- Systematic assessment of family's experiencing parental mental health problems, substance abuse and severe marital conflict or domestic violence should be undertaken routinely to identify the presence of emotionally harmful interactions with the child, and the need for parenting/family support.

Assessment

- Family assessment should include an evaluation of parent–infant/child interaction using standardized and validated tools alongside other aspects of family functioning.

- Assessment of families in which emotionally harmful interactions are taking place should include the impact of such interactions on the child's attachment system and their capacity for trusting relationships; this assessment should inform future intervention.

- An assessment of a family's *capacity for change* should also be implemented using evidence-based tools to evaluate progress.

- The application of evidence-based principles to family assessment (see Chapter 6) would address some of the existing criticisms of the assessment process.

Interventions

- Intervention with families in which parenting is characterized by emotionally harmful interactions or emotional maltreatment should be multimodal and aimed at *bringing about change* across a number of aspects of family functioning including parenting practices, parent–parent and parent–child relationships.

- There is currently limited rigorous evaluation of the effectiveness of interventions explicitly addressing emotional maltreatment but cognitive-behavioural approaches appear to be effective with some parents.

- Other potentially beneficial approaches that have been identified include video-interaction guidance and parent–child psychotherapy.

Service delivery

- There is a need for better coordination and communication between adult mental health and children's services to ensure that children living within *stressful family environments* receive appropriate assessment and support.

- Systematic and flexible approaches to the implementation of evidence-based practices and evidence-informed programmes are needed; this requires greater attention to programme planning, delivery and organization within children's services more generally.

- Many existing methods of working with families (e.g. parenting and home visiting programmes) could include adjunctive components of the type highlighted by this review (i.e. explicitly targeting emotionally harmful parenting) to make them appropriate for emotionally maltreating families.

Research

- More research is needed explicitly evaluating the effectiveness of interventions in improving emotionally harmful and abusive interactions.

- A wide range of *existing interventions* may have an impact on emotionally harmful and abusive interactions and further attention should be given to the potential of such interventions to impact this aspect of parenting, for example home visiting programmes; parenting programmes; family therapy, etc., and evaluation of their effectiveness in improving this outcome.

- More systematic application of terminology relating to emotional maltreatment is needed.

- A number of new methods of working with families experiencing problems such as substance abuse, are being developed that are explicitly aimed at improving parenting. Further development of interventions to support the parenting of parents with mental health problems and severe marital conflict/violence is needed.

Appendix 1
Methods

The following search strategy was implemented, aimed at identifying as many relevant studies as possible.

1. Search strategy

1.1 Databases searched

A thorough search was undertaken of the following databases: Medline; EMBASE; Biological Abstract; PsychINFO; Sociofile; Social Science Citation Index; CINAHL; Dissertation Abstracts; ERIC; Psychological Abstracts; Campbell Collaboration, etc. The objective was to generate as comprehensive a list as possible of primary studies, both published and unpublished.

Unpublished studies were identified using the following sources: NSPCC library and database, Cochrane Library, Current Controlled Trials, National Research Register (NRR) and the Register of the Medical Editors Trial Amnesty. Twenty-five leading researchers in the field were contacted as well as the major national and international child abuse and emergency medical organizations. Reference lists of articles identified through database searches and bibliographies of systematic and non-systematic review articles were examined to identify further relevant studies. A hand search of the contents of the main child abuse journals (*Child Abuse and Neglect; Child Abuse Review; Child Maltreatment; Journal of Emotional Abuse*) was undertaken.

1.2 Inclusion criteria

The following inclusion criteria were used:

1.2.1 Population

Studies were eligible for inclusion in the review if the intervention has been provided directly to parents of children aged 0–19 years, or to both parents and children within that age band. Programmes aimed solely at the treatment of children were not included in the review.

- Prevention programmes were eligible if a specific group at risk for emotional abuse was identified with specified criteria for identification and selection of those at risk.

- Treatment programmes were eligible if they included parents or children in whom emotional abuse has been identified according to any of the definitions outlined above.

- Interventions with parents of children with failure to thrive, parents who were addicted to drugs or alcohol, and parents with severe mental illness were included if the intervention measured changes in parenting.

1.2.2 Interventions

Studies evaluating any intervention that is directed at the secondary prevention or treatment of the following consistent parenting behaviours were included (Glaser and Prior 2002):

- emotional unavailability, unresponsiveness and neglect

- negative attributions and misattributions

- developmentally inappropriate or inconsistent interactions with the child

- failure to recognize the child's individuality and psychological boundary

- failure to promote the child's social adaptation.

1.2.3 Outcomes

Only studies that had measured the following outcomes were included in the review: the impact of the intervention on emotionally abusive parenting using either parent- or child-report standardized measures or independent observations of the following: (i) parental attitudes and (ii) parental behaviour (iii) family functioning and/or (iv) the child's social, emotional, physical and developmental wellbeing and functioning. Diagnostic assessments by clinicians of emotional abuse, children's cognitive, motor, emotional and social development, children's physical health were also included.

1.2.4 Language, time period

Studies that had been published in any of the following languages were included: English, German, French and Spanish. Searches covering the period 1980 to 2007 inclusive were undertaken.

The followings types of studies were excluded: universal primary prevention for vulnerable populations (e.g. poor, single, adolescent mothers) where there has been no clearly identified risk of emotional abuse; treatment in situations where emotional abuse has been enmeshed with physical violence or sexual abuse, or in which physical neglect is the primary presenting problem; interventions that involve identified emotional abuse of children but do not measure change in parent–child emotional interaction. Some, which approximate our inclusion criteria, have been listed with excluded studies (Appendix 2). Interventions that only measure change in risk factors, such as parental depression (Beardslee et al. 2003), insensitivity and troubled attachment have been the subject of recent reviews (such as Bakermans-Kranenburg et al. 2003) that are listed with other excluded studies. Studies of interventions with caregivers who have severe mental illness (SMI) could only be included if change in parenting practices was measured.

Titles and abstracts of studies identified through searches were reviewed to determine whether they met the inclusion criteria (Table Appx 1.1). Abstracts that did not meet the inclusion criteria were rejected. Two independent reviewers assessed full copies of papers that appeared to meet the inclusion criteria. Uncertainties concerning the appropriateness of studies for inclusion in the review were resolved through consultation with a third reviewer.

1.2.5 Search terms

The search terms used to identify relevant studies were adapted for use in the different databases. The search terms used were developed using Glaser and Prior's (2002) definition of emotional abuse (Table Appx 1.1 below).

Table Appx 1.1 Search terms

Child/infant/adolescent child$ or boy$ or girl$ or baby or babies or infant$ or teen$ or adolescen$ or pre school$ or pre-school$ or preschool$ or schoolchild$
Parents mother$ or father$ or parent$ or maternal or paternal or family or families
Abuse emotion$ or psychological or verbal$ adj3 abuse$ or maltreat$ or violen$ or neglect$ or unavailab$ or hostil$ reject$ or spurn$ or abandon$ or denigrate$ or degrade$ or terror$ or isolat$ or missattribute$ or scapegoat$ or hostage or threat$ or withdraw$ or abandon$ unrealistic$ adj3 expectation$ or developmental$ adj3 inconsist$ or developmental$ adj3 inappropriate$ failure to thrive or NOFTT or faltering growth
Treatment intervention$ or prevent$ or treat$ or therap$ or counsel$ or program$ or manage$ or train$ or consult$ or conference$ or support or service$ or parent program$ or parent$ train$ or parent$ education$ or parent$ promotion or parent$-train$ or parent$-program$ or parent$-education$ cognitiv$ adj3 therap$ or train$ behavio#r adj3 therap$ or train$ parent$ adj3 train$ family therap$

No methodological terms were included to ensure that all relevant papers were retrieved. The final search strategies were developed by an iterative process that sought high sensitivity, and excluded no particular study type, since the initial scoping searches indicated that the total volume of relevant literature is limited.

2. Critical appraisal and data extraction

Data was extracted by the lead author, using a data extraction form, and confirmed by the second author. Where data were not available in the published study reports, authors were contacted to supply missing information.

Critical appraisal of the included studies was carried out independently by two authors. Disagreements were discussed and resolved by consensus among reviewers. Where disagreement was due to a lack of information, the authors of a study were contacted for clarification. The scientific rigour of published studies was evaluated according to established guidelines (Centre for Reviews and Dissemination 2009) to inform the interpretation of findings and recommendations for future research (Table Appx 1.2).

Table Appx 1.2 Data extraction criteria

Intervention	Evaluation
Aims Theoretical background Population and setting Intervention content and delivery	Design Identification, allocation and characteristics of subjects Outcomes measured and timing Measure content, reliability and validity Loss to follow-up Analysis and statistical tests used Results Cost information Author's conclusions Assessment of study quality Reviewer's comments

3. Data synthesis

The interventions and outcomes evaluated in the included studies were too diverse to allow for a quantitative synthesis of the study findings. A narrative synthesis is provided, and included studies were classified using the following criteria: aims and outcomes; content and delivery; and implementation.

Quality assessment criteria:

- description of aims and outcomes
- description and number of subjects
- method of allocating subjects and comparability of groups
- description of implementation and integrity of implementation
- loss to follow-up and how accounted for
- description of outcome measures, and data about their validity and reliability
- clarity and precision of analysis and results.

Appendix 2
Key Findings from Included studies

Table Appx 2.1 Evidence from Chapter 5: Parent-focused interventions

Parent-focused interventions		
Study ID	**Measures**	**Results**
Evidence Level A – Randomized controlled trials		
Luthar *et al.* (2007)		Effect size (d) Post-intervention	Effect size (d) 6-month follow-up
	Child maltreatment risk – mother reported – child reported	.10 .60	.60 .74
	Maternal functioning (clinician reported)	.17	.02
	Maternal opiate use Maternal cocaine use	.92 .06	.83 .53
	Child reported – maladjustment Child reported – depression	.02 .04	.02 .12
	Maternal depression Parenting satisfaction Affective quality of parenting Child maladjustment (mother reported)	.10 .77 .69 .99	.28 .31 .48 .72
Luthar and Suchman (2000)		Effect size (significance) Post-intervention	Effect size (significance) 6-month follow-up
	Mother's maltreatment risk Affective interaction Instrumental interaction – limit setting – autonomy Children's perceptions of riskt	.54 (p<0.05) .94 (p<0.001) .08 (n/s) .13 (n/s) .88 (p<0.05)	.57 (p<0.05) .54 (p<0.05) .20 (n/s) .33 (n/s) .27 (n/s)
	Parenting satisfaction Parenting support Depression Child adjustment	.49 (p<0.05) .00 (n/s) .36 (p<.10 – one tailed) .29 (n/s)	.35 (n/s) .21 (n/s) .28 (n/s) .45 (p<.10 – one tailed)
	Children's perceptions re – clinical maladjustment – personal adjustment – school adjustment	.22 (n/s) .53 (p<.10 – one tailed) .22 (n/s)	.39 (n/s) .25 (n/s) .00 (n/s)

Dawe and Harnett (2007)	Parenting Stress Index – total	p<.01
	Child abuse potential – abuse score – rigidity	p<.001 p<0.05
	Parental methadone dose	p<0.05
	Child behaviour Strengths and Difficulties Questionnaire (SDQ): problem score – SDQ prosocial	p<0.01 p=0.05
Black et al. (1995)	Parent–infant interaction at 1 year	No significant between-group differences
	Parental warmth	No significant between-group differences
	Parental control during feeding	Increased similarly across both groups (p=0.01)
	Home environment, including mother's emotional and verbal responsiveness at 1 year	Improvement in overall home environment (p=.05) of children in the home intervention
	Infant weight for age	No significant between-group differences
	Infant weight for height	No significant between-group differences
	Infant height for weight	No significant between-group differences
	Infant cognitive development	Significant decline for all children (p<.001); younger children in home intervention declined less than younger children in clinic only group
	Infant expressive and receptive language development	Significant decline for all children (p<.001), but less so in home intervention than clinic only group (p=0.05)
	Height for age Body Mass Index	n/s difference between home intervention and clinic only p<.10 favouring home intervention
	IQ Reading standard score Arithmetic standard score	n/s difference between home intervention and clinic only n/s difference between home intervention and clinic only n/s difference between home intervention and clinic only
	Behaviour (home) – Internalizing behaviour – Externalizing behaviour	 n/s difference between home intervention and clinic only n/s difference between home intervention and clinic only

Black *et al.* (1995) *cont.*	Behaviour (school) – internalizing behaviour – externalizing behaviour – works hard – behaves appropriately – learning – happy – overall positive classroom behaviour	p<.10 favouring home intervention n/s difference between home intervention and clinic only p<.05 favouring home intervention n/s difference between home intervention and clinic only p<.10 favouring home intervention p<.10 favouring home intervention n/s difference between home intervention and clinic only
Sanders *et al.* (2004)		Group 1 (EBFI) vs. Group 2 (SBFI) interaction at pre- post- and 6-month follow-up
	Blame and intentionality attributions – ambiguous situations – intentional situations	p<.01 favouring Enhanced Behavioural Family Intervention (EBFI) p<.01 favouring Enhanced Behavioural Family Intervention (EBFI)
	Global anger STAXI – angry temperament – anger out – anger expression	n/s difference between Standard Behavioural Family Intervention (SBFI) and EBFI n/s difference between SBFI and EBFI n/s difference between SBFI and EBFI
	Parental anger – problem – intensity	n/s difference between SBFI and EBFI n/s difference between SBFI and EBFI
	Potential for abuse	p<.01 favouring Enhanced Behavioural Family Intervention (EBFI)
	Parent Opinion Questionnaire (POQ), total score	p<.01 favouring Enhanced Behavioural Family Intervention (EBFI)
	Child Abuse Potential Inventory (CAPI), abuse score	p<.01 favouring Enhanced Behavioural Family Intervention (EBFI)
	Parental adjustment – Parent Problem Checklist (PPC) – Depression Stress and Anxiety Scale (DSAS) total score	n/s difference between SBFI and EBFI n/s difference between SBFI and EBFI
	Parenting	n/s difference between SBFI and EBFI
	Parenting Sense of Competency (PSOC) – satisfaction – efficacy	n/s difference between SBFI and EBFI n/s difference between SBFI and EBFI
	Child Behaviour (Eyberg Child Behaviour Checklist) – intensity – problem	n/s difference between SBFI and EBFI n/s difference between SBFI and EBFI

Sanders *et al.* (2004) *cont.*	Parenting Daily Record (PDR) mean problem score) – observed positive child behaviour % – observed negative child behaviour % – child behavioural settings	n/s difference between SBFI and EBFI n/s difference between SBFI and EBFI n/s difference between SBFI and EBFI
	Home and Community Problem Checklist (HCPC) – home problems – community settings	n/s difference between SBFI and EBFI n/s difference between SBFI and EBFI

Evidence Level B – Non-randomized controlled studies

Study ID	Measures	Results
Iwaniec (1997)	22 emotionally abusive behaviours: ratings for behavioural goals collapsed into global categories of satisfactory/improved, moderately improved and no improvement	Combined group showed more reductions in emotionally abusive behaviours (p<0.01)
	Child's reactive and proactive behaviours: Social worker's observations of mother–child interactions.	90% reduction of highly negative behaviour in children in home-only group, 100% in combined intervention (n/s)
	State-Trait anxiety: The State-Trait Anxiety Inventory.	Significant reduction of State anxiety (p<.001) and Trait anxiety (p<.001) for both groups
	Personal parenting stress ratings: parents rated levels of personal stress on a Likert scale at the beginning and end of each session.	Significant reduction of stress levels for both groups (p<.001)

Evidence Level C – One group pre- and post-measures

Study ID	Measures	Results
Knight *et al.* (2007)	Parenting behaviour – non-coercive discipline – coercive discipline – expressive communication – attentive communication – encouragement – clear instruction – inappropriate responses – acceptance/love	Effect size (significance) .40 (n/s) .63 (n/s) .24 (n/s) 0 (n/s) .31 (n/s) .42 (n/s) 1.59 (<0.05) 0 (n/s)

Knight *et al.* (2007) *cont.*	Parenting attitudes	8 out of 16 items showed improved attitudes – effect sizes ranging from 0.3 through to 1.2
Conners *et al.* (2006)	Maternal attitudes associated with child abuse and neglect. – Adult-Adolescent Parenting Inventory – total scale	p<.03
	Subscales – inappropriate expectations of children	p<0.001
	– empathy – strong belief in the use of corporal punishment – reversing parent–child responsibilities – oppressive power over child	n/s n/s p<.01 n/s
	Maternal social functioning, health and mental health – arrest – independent housing – employment – cigarette smoking – depression – post-traumatic stress disorder – needle use scale – risky sexual behaviour scale	p<.001 p<.001 p<.01 p<.01 p<.01 p<.01 p<.001 p<.01
	Drug use	Sig. association between length of stay and relapse, with longer stays associated with abstinence p<.006

Evidence Level D – Retrospective quantitative study

Study ID	Measures	Results
Palusci *et al.* (2008)	Parenting attitudes (AAPI) – expectations – empathy – corporal punishment – roles – independence	p<0.01 p<0.01 p<0.01 n/s n/s

Table Appx 2.2 Results from studies in Chapter 6: Parent–child-focused interventions

Parent–child-focused interventions		
Evidence Level A – Randomized controlled trials		
Study ID	**Measures**	**Statistical significance**
Cicchetti, Rogosch and Toth (2006)	Attachment classification (%)	IPP PPI CS Secure 60.7% 54.5% 1.9% Disorganised 32.1% 45.5% 77.85 [IPP=infant parent psychotherapy; PPI= psychoeducational parenting intervention; CS=community standard control]
	Attachment classification (%)	DI DC NC Insecure to secure 54.3% 7.4% 14.3% [DI=depressed intervention group; DC=depressed control group; NC=non-depressed control group]
Toth *et al.* (2002)	Child's representations of mother – adaptive maternal representations – maladaptive maternal representations	No significant differences between groups PPP showed significant decrease (p<0.001) [PPP=Preschooler Parent Psychotherapy; CS= Community standard control group; PHV=Psychoeducational Home Visitation; NC=Non-maltreated controls]
	Child self-representations – positive self-representations – negative self-representations – false self-representations – mother–child relationship expectations	PPP and CS showed significant increases (p<0.01) PPP group only showed significant decline (p<0.01) No significant between-group differences PPP and PHV showed significant increases (p<0.001 and p<0.01 respectively)
Benoit *et al.* (2001)	Maternal 'atypical' behaviour: communication errors, role reversal, frightening/disoriented behaviour, intrusive and negative behaviour, withdrawal	Significant reduction in play-focused group (p<.02), primarily attributable to a sig. decrease in atypical behaviours from pre- to post-intervention (p<.01). Atypical behaviours in the feeding-focused group remained stable (p<.75).
	Levels of disruptive communication	Significant decrease in atypical behaviours in the play-focused group from pre- to post-intervention (p<.002). Atypical behaviours continued in the feeding-focused group and remained stable pre- to post-intervention (p<.21)

Evidence Level C – One group pre- and post-design		
Study ID	**Measures**	**Statistical significance**
Suchman *et al.* (2008)	Maternal representations of toddler – representational balance	Effect size (d) (significance) 0.29 (p=.02)
	Maternal attributions of toddler: – negative – positive	0.24 (p=.23) 0.30 (p=.43)
	Maternal reflective functioning	0.48 (p=.10)
	Maternal behaviour – sensitivity to cues – response to distress – social/emotional growth fostering – cognitive growth fostering – teaching score – mother contingency	0.57 (p=.09) 0.79 (p=.13) 1.03 (p=.03) 1.18 (p=.01) 1.57 (p=.001) 0.84 (p=.15)
	Maternal psychological adjustment – depression – psychiatric distress – state anxiety – trait anxiety	-1.74 (p=.11) -0.28 (p=.29) 0.27 (p=.26) -0.32 (p=.39)
	Maternal drug abuse – % positive urine toxicology screens	1.13 (p=0.3)
Dunitz *et al.* (1996)	Infant weight/length and growth	All infants achieved normal physical growth. Improvement sig. associated with intervention p<.00001
	Parental Axis 1 psychopathology (depressive disorders, brief reactive psychosis, dysthymnia, somatoform disorders, reactive attachment disorder, alcohol dependence, impulse control, gender identity disorder and sedative dependent disorder).	Pre- During 1 year intervention treatment 70% 37% 12%
	Parental Axis 2 psychopathology (over-involvement, under-involvement, anxious-tense and mixed relationship diagnosis).	24% 24% 18%

References

Allen, B. (2008) 'An analysis of the impact of diverse forms of childhood psychological maltreatment on emotional adjustment in early adulthood.' *Child Maltreatment 13*, 3, 307–312.

American Professional Society on the Abuse of Children (APSAC) (1995) *Guidelines for Psychosocial Evaluation of Suspected Psychological Maltreatment in Children and Adolescents.* Chicago, IL: American Professional Society on the Abuse of Children.

Aosved, A.C. and Long, P.J. (2005) 'College women's experiences of psychological maltreatment and sexual assault.' *Violence and Victims 20*, 5, 577–587.

Asen, E. (2002) 'Outcome research in family therapy.' *Advances in Psychiatric Treatment 8*, 3, 230–238.

Axford, N. (2009) *Defining and Classifying Children in Need.* Aldershot: Ashgate.

Bakermans-Kranenburg, M.J., Juffer, E. and van IJzendoorn, M.H. (1998) ' Interventions with video feedback and attachment discussions: Does type of maternal insecurity make a difference?' *Infant Mental Health Journal 19*, 2, 202–219.

Bakermans-Kranenburg, M.J., van IJzendoorn, M.H. and Juffer, F. (2003) 'Less is more: Meta-analyses of sensitivity and attachment interventions in early childhood.' *Psychological Bulletin 129*, 2, 195–215.

Barlow, J., Coren, E. and Stewart-Brown, S. (2002) 'Meta-analysis of the effectiveness of parenting programmes in improving maternal psychosocial health.' *British Journal Of General Practice (Print), 52*, 476, 223–233.

Barlow, J. and Underdown, A. (2008) 'Supporting Parenting during Infancy.' In C. Jackson, K. Hill and P. Lavis (eds) *Child and Adolescent Mental Health Today: A Handbook.* London: Mental Health Foundation.

Barlow, J. and Svanberg, S. (2009) K*eeping the Baby in Mind: Infant Mental Health in Practice.* London: Routledge.

Bandura, A. (1976) *Social Learning Theory.* Englewood Cliffs, NJ: Prentice Hall.

Barkley, R.A., Edwards, G., Laneri, M., Fletcher, M. and Metevia, L. (2001) 'The efficacy of problem-solving communication training alone, behaviour management training alone, and their combination for parent–adolescent conflict in teenagers with ADHD and ODD.' *Journal of Consulting and Clinical Psychology 69*, 926–941.

Barnett, O., Miller-Perrin, C. and Perrin, R. (eds) (2005) *Family Violence across the Lifespan.* Thousand Oaks, CA: Sage Publications.

Barudy, J. (1998) *El dolor invisible de la infancia: Una lectura ecosistémica del maltrato infantil.* Barcelona: Paidos.

Bateman, A. and Fonagy, P. (2004) *Psychotherapy for Borderline Personality Disorder: Mentalization-based Treatment.* Oxford: Oxford University Press.

Baumrind, D. (1994) 'The social context of child maltreatment.' *Family Relations 43*, 4, 360–368.

Bavolek, S.J. and Keene, G.R. (1999) A*dult–Adolescent Parenting Inventory 2 (AAPI-2).* Park City, UT: Family Development Resources Inc.

Beardslee, W.R., Bemporad, J., Keller, M.B. and Klerman, G.L. (1983) 'Children of parents with major affective disorder: A review.' *American Journal of Psychiatry 140*, 7, 825–832.

Beardslee, W.R., Gladstone, T.R., Wright, E.J. and Cooper, A.B. (2003) 'A family-based approach to the prevention of depressive symptoms in children at risk: Evidence of parental and child change.' *Pediatrics 112*, 2, 119–131.

Behl, L., Conyngham, H. and May, P. (2003) 'Trends in child maltreatment literature.' *Child Abuse and Neglect 27*, 2, 215–229.

Belsky, J. (1993) 'Etiology of child maltreatment: A developmental-ecological analysis.' *Psychological Bulletin 114*, 3, 413–434.

Belt, R. and Punamaki, R.L. (2007) 'Mother–infant group psychotherapy as an intensive treatment in early interaction among mothers with substance abuse problems.' *Journal of Child Psychotherapy 33*, 2, 202–220.

Benoit, D., Madigan, S., Lecce, S., Shea, B. and Goldberg, S. (2001) 'Atypical maternal behavior toward feeding-disordered infants before and after intervention.' *Infant Mental Health Journal 22*, 6, 611–626.

Bifulco, A. and Moran, P. (1998) *Wednesday's Child: Research into Women's Experience of Neglect and Abuse in Childhood and Adult Depression*. London: Routledge.

Binggeli, N. Hart, S. and Brassard, M. (2001) *Psychological Maltreatment of Children*. Thousand Oaks, CA: Sage

Biringen, Z. (2000) 'Emotional availability: Conceptualization and research findings.' *American Journal of Orthopsychiatry 70*, 104–114.

Black, M.M., Dubowitz, H., Hutcheson, J., Berenson-Howard, J. and Starr, R. (1995) 'A randomized clinical trial of home intervention for children with failure to thrive.' *Pediatrics 95*, 6, 807–814.

Black, M.M., Dubowitz, H., Krishnakumar, A. and Starr, R. (2007) 'Early intervention and recovery among children with failure to thrive: Follow-up at age 8.' *Pediatrics 120*, 1, 59–69.

Black, D.A., Heyman, R.E. and Slep, A.M. (2001) 'Risk factors for child physical abuse.' *Aggression and Violent Behaviour 6*, 121–188.

Boulton, S. and Hindle, D. (2000) 'Emotional abuse: The work of a multidisciplinary consultation group in a child psychiatric service.' *Clinical Child Psychology and Psychiatry 5*, 3, 439–452.

Bowlby, J. (1988) *A Secure Base: Parent–Child Attachment and Healthy Human Development*. New York: Basic Books.

Brassard, M.R. and Donovan, K.M. (2006) 'Defining Psychological Maltreatment.' In M. Feerick, J.F. Knutson, P.K.Trickett and S. Flanzer (eds) *Child Abuse and Neglect*. Baltimore, MD: Brookes Publishing.

Bretherton, I., Oppenheim, D., Buchsbaum, H., Emde, R. and The MacArthur Narrative Group (1990) *MacArthur Story-Stem Battery*. University of Wisconsin-Madison. Unpublished manual.

Bretherton, I., Ridgeway, D. and Cassidy, J. (1990) 'Assessing Internal Working Models of the Attachment Relationship: An Attachment Story Completion Task for 3 Year Olds.' In M. Greenberg, D. Ciccetti and E.M. Commings (eds) *Attachment in the Preschool Years*. Chicago, IL: University of Chicago Press.

Bronfman, E.T., Parsons, E. and Lyons-Ruth, K. (1999) Atypical Maternal Behavior Instrument for Assessment and Classification (AMBIANCE). *Manual for coding disrupted affective communication*. Boston, MA: Harvard Medical School. Unpublished Manuscript.

Bull, J., McCormick, G., Swann, C. and Mulvihill, C. (2004) 'Ante-natal and Post-natal Home-visiting Programmes: A Review of Reviews.' *Evidence Briefing*, 1st edn. London: Health Development Agency.

Bumbarger, P. and Perkins, D. (2008). 'After randomised trials: Issues related to the dissemination of evidence-based interventions.' *Journal of Childen's Services 3*, 2, 55–64.

Byng-Hall, J. (2002) 'Relieving parentified children's burdens in families with insecure attachment patterns.' *Family Process 41*, 3, 375–388.

Calder, M.C. and Hackett, S. (eds) (2003) *Assessment in Childcare: Using and Developing Frameworks for Practice*. Dorset: Russell House Publishing.

Cassidy, J. and Shaver, P.R (eds) (2008) *Handbook of Attachment: Theory, Research, and Clinical*

Carr, A. (2006) 'Thematic review of family therapy journals in 2005.' *Journal of Family Therapy 28*, 4, 420–439.

Cassidy, J., Woodhouse, S.S., Cooper, G., Hoffman, K., Powell, B. and Rodenberg, M. (2005) 'Examination of the Precursors of Infant Attachment Security: Implications for Early Intervention and Intervention Research.' In L.J. Berlin, Y. Ziv, L. Amaya-Jackson and M.T. Greenberg (eds) *Enhancing Early Attachments: Theory, Research, Intervention and Policy*. London: Guilford Press.

Cawson, P., Wattam, C., Brooker, S. and Kelly, G. (2000) *Child Maltreatment in the United Kingdom: A Study of the Prevalence of Child Abuse and Neglect.* London: NSPCC.

Centre for Reviews and Dissemination (2009) *Systematic Reviews: CRD's guidance for undertaking reviews in health care.* York: CRD.

Chaffin, M., Kelleher, K. and Hollenberg, J. (1996) 'Onset of physical abuse and neglect: Psychiatric substance abuse and social risk factors from prospective community data.' *Child Abuse and Neglect 20*, 3, 191–203.

Chirichella-Besemer, D. and Motta, R. (2008) 'Psychological maltreatment and its relationship with negative affect in men and women.' *Journal of Emotional Abuse 8*, 4, 423–445.

Cicchetti, D, and Carlson, V. (eds) (1995) *Child Maltreatment: Theory and research on the causes and consequences of child abuse and neglect.* Cambridge: Cambridge University Press.

Cicchetti, D. and Lynch, M. (1993) 'Toward an ecological/transactional model of community violence and child maltreatment: Consequences for children's development.' *Psychiatry 56*, 1, 96–118.

Cicchetti, D. and Rizley, R. (1981) 'Developmental perspective on the etiology, intergenerational transmission and sequelae of child maltreatment.' *New Directions for Child Development 11*, 31–55.

Cicchetti, D., Rogosch, F.A. and Toth, S.L. (2006) 'Fostering secure attachment in infants in maltreating families through preventive interventions.' *Development and Psychopathology 18*, 623–649.

Cirillo, S. and di Blasio, P. (1998) *Niños maltratados.* Barcelona: Paidós Ibérica.

Cleaver, H. and Walker, S. (2004) 'From policy to practice: The implementation of a new framework for social work assessments of children and families.' *Child and Family Social Work 9*, 1, 81–90.

Cohen, N., Lojkasek, M., Muir, E., Muir, R. and Parker, C. (2000) 'Six-month follow-up of two mother–infant psychotherapies.' *Infant Mental Health Journal 23*, 4, 361–380.

Cohen, N.J., Muir, E., Lojkasek, M., Muir, R. *et al.* (1999) 'Watch, wait and wonder: Testing the effectiveness of a new approach to mother–infant psychotherapy.' *Infant Mental Health Journal 20*, 4, 429–451.

Conley, C. (2003) 'A review of parenting capacity assessment reports.' *Ontario Association of Children's Aid Societies Journal 47*, 16–22.

Conners, N.A., Grant, A., Crone, C.C. and Whiteside-Mansell, L. (2006) 'Substance abuse treatment for mothers: Treatment outcomes and the impact of length of stay.' *Journal of Substance Abuse Treatment 31*, 4, 447–456.

Corby, B. (2003) *Child Abuse: Towards a Knowledge Base.* Buckingham: Open University Press.

Corby, B., Millar, M. and Pope, A. (2002) 'Assessing Children in Need Assessment – A parental perspective.' *Practice 14*, 4, 5–16.

Cowan, P. and Cowan, C.P. (2008) 'Diverging family policies to promote children's well-being in the UK and US: Some relevant data from family research and intervention studies.' *Journal of Children's Services 3*, 4, 4–16.

Coyne, L., Low, C., Miller, A., Seifer, R. and Dickstein, S. (2007) 'Mothers' empathic understanding of their toddlers: Associations with maternal depression and sensitivity.' *Journal of Child and Family Studies 16*, 4, 483–497.

Cramer, B. and Stern, D. (1988) 'Evaluation of changes in mother–infant brief psychotherapy: A single case study.' *Infant Mental Health Journal 9*, 1, 1–73.

Creighton, S. and Russell, N. (1995) *Voices from Childhood: A Survey of Childhood Experiences and Attitudes to Childrearing among Adults in the United Kingdom.* London: NSPCC.

Crittenden, P.M. (1981) 'Abusing, neglecting, problematic, and adequate dyads: Differentiating by patterns of interaction.' *Merrill-Palmer Quarterly 27*, 1–18.

Darlington, Y., Feeney, J. and Rixon, K. (2005) 'Interagency collaboration between child protection and mental health services: Practices, attitudes and barriers.' *Child Abuse and Neglect 29*, 10, 1085–1098.

Davis, H. (2009) 'The Family Partnership Model: Understanding the Process of Prevention and Early Intervention.' In J. Barlow and P.O. Svanberg (eds) *Keeping the Baby in Mind: Infant Mental Health in Practice*. Hove: Routledge.

Davis, H., Day, C. and Bidmead, C. (2002) *Working in Partnership with Parents: The Parent Adviser Model*. London: Harcourt Assessment.

Davis, H. and Spurr, P. (1998) 'Parent counselling: An evaluation of a community child mental health services.' *Journal of Child Psychology and Psychiatry 39*, 365–376.

Dawe, S. and Harnett, P. (2007) 'Reducing potential for child abuse among methadone-maintained parents: Results from a randomized controlled trial.' *Journal of Substance Abuse Treatment 32*, 4, 381–390.

Dawe, S., Harnett, P.H., Rendalls, V. and Staiger, P. (2003) 'Improving family functioning and child outcome in methadone maintained families.' *The Parents Under Pressure Program Drug and Alcohol Review 22*, 299–307.

Department for Children, Schools and Families (2008) *Statistical First Release*. London: HMSO.

Department for Children, Schools and Families (2009) *The Protection of Children in England: Action Plan. The Government's Response to Lord Laming*. London: The Stationery Office.

Department for Education and Skills (2003) *Every Child Matters*. London: HMSO.

Department for Education and Skills (2004) *Every Child Matters: Next Steps*. London: HMSO.

Department for Education and Skills (2007) *Aiming High for Children: Supporting Families*. London: The Stationery Office.

Department of Health (1995) *Children and Young People on Child Protection Registers, Year Ending 31 March 1995*. London: HMSO.

Department of Health (1999) *Working Together to Safeguard Children*. London: HMSO.

Department of Health (2000) *Framework for the Assesment of Children in Need and their Families*. London: HMSO.

Department of Health (2009) *Child Health Promotion Programme – Pregnancy and the First Five Years of Life*. London: Department of Health.

Department of Health and Department for Education and Skills (2004) *Core Standards – National Service Framework for Children, Young People and Maternity Services*. London: Department of Health.

DiCaccavo, A. (2006) 'Working with parentification: Implications for clients and counselling psychologists.' *Psychology and Psychotherapy: Theory, Research and Practice 79*, 3, 469–478.

DiLillo, D., Perry, A.R. and Fortier, M. (2005) 'Child Physical Abuse and Neglect.' In J.C. Thomas and D.L. Segal (eds) *Comprehensive Handbook of Personality and Psychopathology*, Vol. 3. New Jersey: John Wiley.

Doyle, C. (1997) 'Emotional abuse of children: Issues for intervention.' *Child Abuse Review 6*, 5, 330–342.

Dretzke, J., Davenport, C., Frew, E., Barlow, J., Stewart-Brown, S., Bayliss, S., Taylor, R.S., Sandercock, J. and Hyde, C. (2009) 'The clinical effectiveness of different parenting programmes for children with conduct problems: A systematic review of randomised controlled trials.' *BMC Child and Adolescent Psychiatry and Mental Health 3*, 7. Available at www.capmh.com/content/3/1/7, accessed on 7 January 2010.

Dunitz, M., Scheer, P., Trojovsky, A., Kaschnitz, W., Kvas, E. and Macari, S. (1996) 'Changes in psychopathology of parents of NOFT (non-organic failure to thrive) infants during treatment.' *European Child and Adolescent Psychiatry 5*, 2, 93–100.

Durlak, J.A. and DuPre, E.P. (2008) 'Implemenatiion matters: A review of research on the influence of implementation on programme outcomes and the factors affecting the implementation.' *American Journal of Community Psychology 41*, 327–350.

Durrant, J.E. (1999) 'Evaluating the success of Sweden's corporal punishment ban.' *Child Abuse and Neglect 23*, 5, 435–448.

Egeland, B. (2009) 'Taking stock: Child emotional maltreatment and developmental psychopathology.' *Child Abuse and Neglect 33*, 1, 22–26.

Egeland, B., Sroufe, L. and Erickson, M. (1983) 'The developmental consequence of different patterns of maltreatment.' *Child Abuse and Neglect 7*, 4, 459–469.

Egeland, B., Weinfield, N.S., Bosquet, M. and Cheng, V.K. (2000) ' Remembering, Repeating, and Working Through: Lessons from attachment-based interventions.' In J. Osofsky and H.E. Fitzgerald (eds) *WAIMH handbook of infant mental health: Vol 4. Infant mental health in groups at high risk.* New York: Wiley, pp.35–89.

Embry, D.D. and Biglan, A. (2008) 'Evidence-based kernals: Fundamental units of behavioural influence.' *Clinical, Child and Family Psychology Review 11*, 3, 75–113.

Erickson, M., Egeland, B. and Pianta, R. (1989) 'The Effects of Maltreatment on the Development of Young Children.' In D. Cicchetti and V. Carlson (eds) *Child Maltreatment: Theory and Research on the Causes and Consequences of Child Abuse and Neglect.* New York, NY: Cambridge University Press.

Evans, H. (2002) *Emotional Abuse: Research Briefing.* London: NSPCC.

Eyberg, S.N., Besmeer, J., Newcomb, K., Edwards, D. and Robinson, E. (1994) *Manual for the Dyadic Parent–Child Interaction Coding System II.* Social and Behavioural Science Documents (MS2897).

Felitti, V., Anda, R., Nordenberg, D., Williamson, D. *et al.* (1998) 'Relationship of Childhood Abuse and Household Dysfunction to Many of the Leading Causes of Death in Adults: The Adverse Childhood Experiences, ACE study.' *American Journal of Preventive Medicine 14*, 245–258.

Foster, C., Garber, J. and Durlak, J. (2008) 'Current and past maternal depression, maternal interaction behaviors and children's externalizing and internalizing symptoms.' *Journal of Abnormal Child Psychology 36*, 4, 527–537.

Fraiberg, S. (1980) *Clinical Studies in Infant Mental Health.* New York: Basic.

Fraiberg, S.H., Adelson, E. and Shapiro, V.B. (1975) 'Ghosts in the nursery: A psychoanalytic approach to the problem of infant/mother relationships.' *Journal of the American Academy of Child Psychiatry 14*, 3, 386–422.

Fraser, L. (1995) 'Eastfield Ming Quong: Multiple-impact In-home Treatment Model.' In L. Combrick-Graham (ed.) *Children and Families at Risk.* New York, NY: Guilford Press.

Gilbert, R., Kemp, A., Thoburn, J.,Sidebotham, P., Radford, L., Glaser, D. and MacMillan, H. (2009) 'Recognising and responding to child maltreatment.' *The Lancet 373*, 9658, 167–180.

Glaser, D. (2002) 'Emotional abuse and neglect (psychological maltreatment): A conceptual framework. *Child Abuse and Neglect 26*, 6/7, 697–714.

Glaser, D. (1995) 'Emotionally Abusive Experiences.' In P. Reder and C. Lucy (eds) *Assessment of Parenting. Psychiatric and Psychological Contributions.* London: Routledge, pp.73–86.

Glaser, D. and Prior, V. (1997) 'Is the term child protection applicable to emotional abuse?' *Child Abuse Review 6*, 5, 315–329.

Glaser, D., Prior, V. and Lynch, M. (2001) *Emotional Abuse and Emotional Neglect: Antecedents, Operational Definitions and Consequences.* York: BASPCAN.

Glaser, D. and Prior, V. (2002) 'Predicting Emotional Abuse and Neglect.' In K. Browne, H. Hanks, P. Stratton and C. Hamilton (eds) *Early Prediction and Prevention of Child Abuse.* Chichester: Wiley.

Green, J. and Goldwyn, R. (2002) 'Annotation: Attachment disorganisation and psychopathology: new findings in attachment research and their potential implications for developmental psychopathology in childhood.' *Journal of Child Psychology and Psychiatry and Allied Disciplines 43*, 7, 835–846.

Greenberg, M.T., Domitrovich, C.E., Graczyk, P.A. and Sins, J.E. (2005) *The Study of Implementation in School-Based Preventive Interventions: Theory, Research and Practice.* Rockville, MD: Centre for Mental Health Services, Substance Abuse and Mental Health Services Administation. Cited in Axford et al. 2009.

Guedeney, A. and Fermanian, J. (2001) 'A validity and reliability study of assessment and screening for sustained withdrawal reaction in infancy: The Alarm Distress Baby Scale.' *Infant Mental Health Journal 22*, 5, 559–575.

Harnett, P.H. and Dawe, S. (2008) 'Reducing child abuse potential in families identified by social services: Implications for assessment and treatment.' *Brief Treatment and Crisis Intervention 8*, 226 – 235.

Harnett, P. (2007) 'A procedure for assessing parents' capacity for change in child protection cases.' *Children and Youth Services Review 29*, 1179–1188.

Hart, S., Binggeli, N. and Brassard, M. (1998) 'Evidence for the effects of psychological maltreatment.' *Journal of Emotional Abuse 1*, 27–58.

Haynes, R.B., Devereaux, P.J. and Guyatt, G.H. (2002) 'Physicians' and patients' choices in evidence based practice. Evidence does not make decisions, people do.' *British Medical Journal 324*, 1350.

Hill, L.G., Parker, L.A., McGuire, J.K. and Sage, R. (2008) 'Institutionalising science-based practices in children's services.' *Journal of Children Services 3*, 4, 32–45.

Hinden, B., Biebel, K., Nicholson, J., Henry, A. and Katz-Leavy, J. (2006) 'A Survey of Programs for Parents with Mental Illness and their Families: Identifying Common Elements to Build the Evidence Base.' *Journal of Behavioral Health Services and Research 33*, 1, 21–38.

Hoffman, K.T., Margin R.S., Cooper, G. and Powell, B. (2006) 'Changing Toddlers' and Preschoolers' attachment Classifications: The Circle of Security Intervention.' *Journal of Consulting and Clinical Psychology 74*, 6, 1017–1026.

Howe, D. (2005) *Child Abuse and Neglect: Attachment, Development and Intervention*. Basingstoke: Palgrave Macmillan.

Howe, D., Brandon, M., Hinnigs, D. and Schofield, G. (1999) *Attachment Theory, Child Development and Family Support: A Practice and Assessment Model*. Basingstoke: Macmillan.

Hutcheson, J., Black, M.M., Talley, M., Dubowitz, H. *et al.* (1997) 'Risk status and home intervention among children with failure-to-thrive: Follow-up at age 4. *Journal of Pediatric Psychology 22*, 5, 651–668.

Inter-Agency Working Group on Children's Participation (2007) *Children's participation in decision making: Why do it, when to do it, how to do it*. Bangkok: IAWGCP.

Iwaniec, D. (1995) *The Emotionally Abused and Neglected Child: Identification, Assessment and Intervention*. Chichester: John Wiley and Sons.

Iwaniec, D. (1997a) 'Evaluating parent training for emotionally abusive and neglectful parents: Comparing individual versus individual and group intervention.' *Research in Social Work Practice 7*, 3, 329–349.

Iwaniec, D. (1997b) 'An overview of emotional maltreatment and failure-to-thrive.' *Child Abuse Review 6*, 5, 370–388.

Iwaniec, D. (2007) *The Emotionally Abused and Neglected Child: Identification, Assessment and Intervention*. Chichester: John Wiley and Sons.

Iwaniec, D. and Herbert, M. (1999) 'Multi-dimensional approach to helping families who emotionally abuse their children.' *Children and Society 13*, 365–379.

Jacobson, N.S. and Truax, P. (1991) 'Clinical significance: A statistical approach to defining meaningful change in psychopathology research.' *Journal of Consulting and Clinical Psychology 59*, 12–19.

Jacobvitz, D., Hazen, N. and Riggs, S. (1997) 'Disorganized Mental Processes in Mothers, Frightening/Frightened Caregiving and Disorganized Behavior in Infancy.' Paper presented at the meeting of the Society of Research in Child Development, Washington DC, April 1997.

Jaffe, P., Wolfe, D.A. and Wilson, S.K. (1990) *Children of Battered Women*. (Developmental Clinical Psychology and Psychiatry, Vol. 21). Thousand Oaks, CA: Sage Publications.

Katz, I. and Hetherington, R. (2006) 'Co-operating and communicating: a European perspective on integrating services for children.' *Child Abuse Review 15*, 6, 429–439.

Kauffman, C., Grunebaum, H., Cohler, B. and Gamer, E. (1979) Superkids: 'Competent children of psychotic mothers.' *American Journal of Psychiatry 136*, 11, 1398–1402.

Kelly, G. (1991) *The Psychology of Personal Constructs. Vol. 1: A Theory of Personality*. London: Routledge.

Keren, M., Feldman, R. and Tyano, S. (2001) 'Diagnoses and interactive patterns of infants referred to a community-based infant mental health clinic.' *Journal of the American Academy of Child and Adolescent Psychiatry 40*, 27–35.

Kerr, M., Black, M.M. and Krishanakumar, A. (2000) 'Failure to thrive, maltreatment and the behaviour and development of 6-year-old children from low income urban families.' *Child Abuse and Neglect 24*, 5, 587–598.

Knight, D.K., Bartholomew, N.G. and Simpson, D.D. (2007) 'An exploratory study of "Partners in Parenting" within two substance abuse treatment programmes for women.' *Psychological Services 4*, 4, 262–276.

Koenen, K.C., Moffitt, T.E., Caspi, A., Taylor, A. and Purcell, S. (2003) 'Domestic violence is associated with environmental suppression of IQ in young children.' *Developmental Psychopathology 15*, 2, 297–311.

Kolozian, K. (2007) 'Risk Factors, Maternal Depression and Mother–Child Interactions in the National Early Head Start Population.' *Dissertation Abstracts International: Section B: The Sciences and Engineering 68*, 3-B, 1930.

Kotch, J., Lewis, T., Hussey, J., English, D. *et al.* (2008) 'Importance of early neglect for childhood aggression.' *Pediatrics 121*, 4, 725–731.

Lieberman, A.F. (1997) 'Toddlers' Internalization of Maternal Attributions as a Factor in Quality of Attachment.' In L. Atkinson and K. Zucker (eds) *Attachment and Psychopathology*. New York: Guilford Press, pp. 277–299.

Loh, C. and Vostanis, P. (2004) 'Perceived mother–infant relationship difficulties in postnatal depression.' *Infant and Child Development 13*, 2, 159–171.

Lopez-Stane, M.A. (2006) 'Understanding childhood psychological maltreatment in an urban university population.' *Dissertation Abstracts International Section A: Humanities and Social Sciences 67*, 9-A, 3299.

Lord Laming (2003) *The Victoria Climbié Inquiry Report*. London: HMSO.

Lord Laming (2009) *The Protection of Children in England: A Progress Report*. London: The Stationery Office.

Lovejoy, M.C., Graczyk, P.A., O'Hare, E. and Neuman, G. (2000) 'Maternal depression and parenting behaviour: A meta-analytic review.' *Clinical Psychology Review 20*, 5, 561–592.

Luthar, S. and Suchman, N. (2000) 'Relational Psychotherapy Mothers' Group: A developmentally informed intervention for at-risk mothers.' *Development and Psychopathology 12*, 2, 235–253.

Luthar, S., Suchman, N. and Altomare, M. (2007) 'Relational Psychotherapy Mothers' Group: A randomized clinical trial for substance abusing mothers.' *Development and Psychopathology 19*, 1, 243–261.

Lyons-Ruth, K., Yellin, C., Melnick, S. and Atwood, G. (2005) 'Expanding the concept of unresolved mental states: Hostile/Helpless states of mind on the adult attachment interview are associated with atypical maternal behavior and infant disorganization.' *Development and Psychopathology 17*, 1–23.

Mackner, L., Starr, R.H. and Black, M. (1997) 'The cumulative effect of neglect and failure to thrive on cognitive functioning.' *Child Abuse and Neglect 21*, 7, 691–700.

Macdonald, G. (2001) *Effective Interventions for Child Abuse and Neglect*. Chichester: Wiley.

Macdonald, G. and Winkley, A. (1999) *What Works in Child Protection?* Barkingside: Barnardo's.

Main, M. and Hesse, E. (1990) 'Parents' Unresolved Traumatic Experiences are Related to Infant Disorganized Attachment Status: Is Frightened and/or Frightening Parental Behavior the Linking Mechanism?' In M. Greenberg, D. Cicchetti and E. Cummings (eds) *Attachment in the Preschool Years: Theory, Research and Intervention*. Chicago, IL: University of Chicago Press.

Main, M. and Hesse, E.D. (1992). 'Disorganized/disoriented infant behavior in the Strange Situation, lapses in the monitoring of reasoning and discourse during the parent's Adult Attachment Interview, and dissociative states.' In M. Ammaniti and D. Stern *(eds) Attachment and Psychoanalysis*. Gius: Rome, pp.86–140.

Markie-Dadds, C., Turner, K.M.T. and Sanders, M.R. (1997) *Every Parents Group Workbook*. Brisbane, Queensland, Australia: Australian Academic.

McDonough, S. (2000) 'Interaction Guidance: An Approach for Difficult-to-Engage Families.' In C.H. Zeanah, Jr. (ed.) *Handbook of Infant Mental Health*, 2nd edn. London: Guilford Press.

Mikulincer, M., Shaver, P.R. and Pereg, D. (2003) 'Attachment theory and affect regulation: The dynamics, development, and cognitive consequences of attachment-related strategies.' *Motivation and Emotion 27*, 2, 77–102.

Minuchin, S. (1974) *Families and Family Therapy*. Cambridge, MA: Harvard University Press.

Morrell, C.J., Spiby, H., Stewart, P., Walters, S. and Morgan, A. (2000) 'Costs and effectiveness of community postnatal support workers: Randomised controlled trial.' *British Medical Journal 321*, 593–598.

National Centre on Addiction and Substance Abuse (NCASA) (1996) *Substance Abuse and the American Woman*. New York, NY: NCASA.

Newson, J. and Newson, E. (1990) 'The Extent of Physical Punishment in the UK.' (Approach) Paper prepared for the Children's Legal Centre seminar on protecting children and parental physical discipline, University of Nottingham, July 1986.

Nobes, G. and Smith, M. (1995) 'Physical punishment of children in two-parent families.' *Child Psychology and Psychiatry 1997*, 2, 271–281. [year]

O'Hagan, K. (2006) *Identifying Emotional and Psychological Abuse*. Maidenhead: Open University Press.

Olds, D., Henderson, C.R., Cole, R., Eckenrode, J. *et al.* (1998) 'Long-term effects of nurse home visitation on children's criminal and antisocial behavior: 15-year follow-up of a randomized controlled trial.' *Journal of the American Medical Association 280*, 14, 1238–1244.

Palusci, V.J., Crum, P., Bliss, R. and Bavolek, S.J. (2008) 'Changes in parenting attitudes and knowledge among inmates and other at-risk populations after a family nurturing program.' *Children and Youth Services Review 30*, 1, 79–89.

Parton, N. (2004) 'Child Protection and Family Support: Current debates and future prospects.' In N. Parton (ed.) *Child Protection and Family Support: Tensions, Contradictions and Possibilties*. London: Routledge.

Pawlby, S., Marks, M., Clarke, R., Best, E., Weir, D. and O'Keane, V. (2005) 'Mother–infant interaction in postpartum women with severe mental illness (SMI) before and after treatment.' *Archives of Women's Mental Health 8*, 120.

Platt, D. (2001) 'Refocusing children's services: Evaluation of an initial assessment process.' *Child and Family Social Work 6*, 139–148.

Platt, D. (2006) 'Threshold decisions: How social workers prioritize referrals and child concern.' *Child Abuse Review 15*, 4, 4–18.

Prinz, R.J., Sanders, M.R., Shapiro, C.J., Whitaker, D.J. and Lutzker, J.R. (2009) 'Population-based prevention of child maltreatment: The US Triple P system population trial.' *Prevention Science 10*, 1, 1–12.

Robinson, J., Mantz-Simmons, L., Macfie, J. and The MacArthur Narrative Working Group (1996) *The Narrative Coding Manual – Rochester Revision*. Unpublished manuscript.

Rohner, R. and Rohner, E. (1981) 'Parental acceptance-rejection and parental control: Cross-cultural codes.' *Ethnology 20*, 245–260.

Rohner, R. and Rohner, N. (1991) 'Cross-national perspectives on parental acceptance-rejection theory.' *Marriage and Family Review 35*, 3/4, 85–105.

Roldan, M.C., Galera, S. and O'Brien, B. (2005) 'Women living in a drug (and violence) context – the maternal role.' *Revista Latino-Americana de Enfermagem 13*, 2, 1118–1126.

Rose, G. (2001) 'Sick individuals and sick populations.' *International Journal of Epidemiology 30*, 427–432.

Rowe, A. (2009) 'Perinatal Home Visiting: Implementing the Nurse–Family Partnership in England.' In J. Barlow and P.O. Svanberg (eds) *Keeping the Baby in Mind: Infant Mental Health in Practice*. Hove: Routledge.

Rutter, M., Kreppner, J. and Sonuga-Barke, E. (2009) 'Emanuel Miller Lecture: Attachment insecurity, disinhibited attachment, and attachment disorders: Where do research findings leave the concepts?' *Journal of Child Psychology and Psychiatry 50*, 5, 529–543.

Sanders, M. (1999) 'The Triple-P Positive Parenting Program: Towards an empirically validated multilevel parenting support program for the prevention of behavior and emotional problems in children.' *Clinical Child and Family Psychology Review 2*, 71–90.

Sanders, M.R. (2008) 'The Triple P-Positive Parenting Program: A public health approach to parenting support.' *Journal of Family Psychology 22*, 506–517.

Sanders, M., Pidgeon, A., Gravestock, F., Connors, M.D., Brown, S. and Young, R. (2004) 'Does parental attributional retraining and anger management enhance the effects of the Triple P-Positive Parenting Program with parents at risk of child maltreatment?' *Behavior Therapy 35*, 3, 513–535.

Schaffer, A., Yates, T. and Egeland, B. (2009) 'The relation of emotional maltreatment to early adolescent competence: Developmental processes in a prospective study.' *Child Abuse and Neglect 33*, 1, 36–44.

Schore, A. (1994) *Affect Regulation and the Origin of the Self: The Neurobiology of Emotional Development.* Mahwah, NJ: Erlbaum.

Shlonsky, A. and Wagner, D. (2005) 'The next step: Integrating actuarial risk assessment and clinical judgment into an evidence-based practice framework in CPS case management.' *Children and Youth Services Review 27*, 4, 409–427.

Slade, A., Sadler, L., de Dios-Kenn, C., Webb, D., Currier-Ezepchick, J. and Mayes, L. (2005) 'Minding the baby: A reflective parenting program.' *The Psychoanalytic Study of the Child 60*, 74–100.

Small, S.A., Cooney, S.M. and O'Connor, C. (2009) 'Evidence-informed program improvement: Using principles of effectiveness to enhance the quality and impact of family-based prevention programs.' *Family Relation 58*, 1, 1–13.

Social Work Taskforce (2009) *Building a Safe Confident Future: The Final Report of the Social Work Taskforce.* London: HMSO.

Spratt, T. (2001) 'The influence of child protection orientation on child welfare practice.' *British Journal of Social Work 31*, 933–954.

Spratt, T. and Callan, J. (2004) 'Parents' views on social work interventions in child welfare cases.' *British Journal of Social Work 34*, 199–224.

Sroufe, L.A. (2005) 'Attachment and development: A prospective, longitudinal study from birth to adulthood. *Attachment and Human Development 7*, 4, 349–367.

Stanley, C., Murray, L. and Stein, A. (2004) 'The effect of postnatal depression on mother–infant interaction, infant response to the still-face perturbation and performance on an instrumental learning task.' *Development and Psychopathology 16*, 1, 1–18.

Steadman, J., Pawlby, S., Mayers, A., Bucks, R. *et al.* (2007) 'An exploratory study of the relationship between mother–infant interaction and maternal cognitive function in mothers with mental illness.' *Journal of Reproductive and Infant Psychology 25*, 4, 255–269.

Steele, B. and Pollack, C. (1968) 'A Psychiatric Study of Parents who Abuse Infants and Small Children.' In R. Helfer and C. Kempe (eds) *The Battered Child Syndrome.* Chicago, IL: University of Chicago Press.

Stern, D. (1998) The Interpersonal World of the Infant: A View from Psychoanalysis and Development. New York, NY: Basic Books.

Stratton, P. (2005) *Report on the Evidence Base of Systemic Family Therapy.* Warrington: The Association of Family Therapy. Available at www.aft.org.uk/docs/evidencedocsept05creditedSS.doc, accessed on 22 August 2009.

Straussner, S.L.A. and Fewell, C.H. (2006) 'Preface.' *Journal of Social Work Practice in the Addictions 6*, 1/2, xxi–xxviii.

Sturge-Apple, M.L., Davies, P.T. and Cummings, E.M. (2006) 'Hostility and withdrawal in marital conflict: Effects on parental emotional unavailability and inconsistent discipline.' *Journal of Family Psychology 20*, 2, 227–238.

Suchman, N., Legow, N., DeCoste, C., Castiglioni, N. and Mayes, L. (2008) 'The Mothers and Toddlers Program: Preliminary findings from an attachment-based parenting intervention for substance-abusing mothers.' *Psychoanalytic Psychology 25*, 3, 499–517.

Svanberg, P.O. (2009) 'Promoting a Secure Attachment through Early Screening and Interventions: A partnership Approach.' In J. Barlow and P.O. Svanberg (eds) *Keeping the Baby in Mind: Infant Mental Health in Practice.* Hove: Routledge.

Teicher, M., Samson, J., Polcari, A. and McGreenery, C. (2006) 'Sticks, stones and hurtful words: Relative effects of various forms of childhood maltreatment.' *American Journal of Psychiatry 163*, 6, 993–1000.

Toth, S., Maughan, A., Todd Manly, J., Spagnola, M. and Cicchetti, C. (2002) 'The relative efficacy of two interventions in altering maltreated preschool children's representational models: Implications for attachment theory.' *Development and Psychopathology 14*, 887–908.

Toth, S.L., Rogosch, F.A., Cicchetti, D., Manly, J.T. (2006) 'The efficacy of toddler–parent psychotherapy to reorganise attachment in the young offspring of mothers with major depressive disorder: A randomised preventive trial.' *Journal of Consulting and Clinical Psychology 74*, 6.

Trapolini, T., Ungerer, J. and McMahon, C. (2008) 'Maternal depression: Relations with maternal caregiving representations and emotional availability during the preschool years.' *Attachment and Human Development 10*, 1, 73–90.

Trickett, P., Mennen, F., Kim, K. and Sang, J. (2009) 'Emotional abuse in a sample of multiply maltreated, urban young adolescents: Issues of definition and identification.' *Child Abuse and Neglect 33*, 1, 27–35.

Turner, S., Beidel, D., Roberson-Nay, R. and Tervo, K. (2003) 'Parenting behaviors in parents with anxiety disorders.' *Behaviour Research and Therapy 41*, 5, 541–554.

Van IJzendoorn, M.H. and Bakermans-Kranenburg, M.J. (1997) 'Intergenerational Transmission of Attachment: A move to the contextual level.' In L. Atkinson and K.J. Zucker (eds) *Attachment and Psychopathology.* New York: Guilford, pp. 135–170.

Volpe, J. (1996) *Effects of Domestic Violence on Children and Adolescents: An Overview.* Commack, NY: American Academy of Experts in Traumatic Stress.

Wan, M., Salmon, M., Riordan, D., Appleby, L., Webb, R. and Abel, K.M. (2007) 'What predicts poor mother–infant interaction in schizophrenia?' *Psychological Medicine 37*, 4, 537–546.

Ward, H., Holmes, L., Moyers, S., Munro, E.R. and Poursanidou, D. (2004) *Safeguarding Children: A Scoping Study of Research in Three Areas.* Loughborough: Centre for Child and Family Research.

Webb, M., Heisler, D., Call, S., Chickering, S. and Colburn, T. (2007) 'Shame, guilt, symptoms of depression and reported history of psychological maltreatment.' *Child Abuse and Neglect 31*, 11/12, 1143–1153.

Webster-Stratton, C. and Hammond, M. (1990) 'Predictors of treatment outcome in parent training for families with conduct problem children.' *Behavior Therapy 21*, 319–337.

Webster-Stratton, C., Hollinsworth, T. and Kopacoff, M. (1989) 'The long-term effectiveness and clinical significance of three cost-effective training programs for families with conduct-problem children.' *Journal of Consulting and Clinical Psychology 57*, 550–553.

Wekerle, C., Leung, E., Wall, A.M., MacMillan, H. *et al.* (2009) 'The contribution of childhood emotional abuse to teen dating violence among child protective services involved youth.' *Child Abuse and Neglect 33*, 1, 45–58.

What Works, Wisconsin (2007) *Family Living Programs.* Madison, WI: University of Wisconsin. Available at www.uwex.edu/ces/flp/families/whatworks.cfm, accessed on 1 September 2008.

Wilding, J. and Thoburn, J. (1997) 'Family support plans for neglected and emotionally maltreated children.' Child Abuse Review 6, 5, 343–356. Cited in Evans, H. (2002) *Emotional abuse: research briefing.* London: NSPCC.

Witkiewitz, K. and Dodge-Reyome, N. (2001) 'Recollections of childhood psychological maltreatment and self-reported eating disordered behaviors in undergraduate college females.' *Journal of Emotional Abuse 2*, 1, 15–29.

Wolfe, D., Crooks, C., Lee, V., McIntyre-Smith, A. and Jaffe, P. (2003) 'The effects of children's exposure to domestic violence: A meta-analysis and critique.' *Clinical, Child and Family Psychological Review 6*, 3, 171–187.

Wooster, D. (1999) 'Assessment of nonorganic failure to thrive.' *Infant-Toddler Intervention: The Transdisciplinary Journal 9*, 4, 353–371.

World Health Organization (2002) *World Report on Violence and Health.* Geneva: WHO. Available at www.who.int/violence_injury_prevention/violence/world_report/en, accessed 26 August 2009.

Wright, M., Crawford, E. and Del Castillo, D. (2009) 'Childhood emotional maltreatment and later psychological distress among college students: The mediating role of maladaptive schemas.' *Child Abuse and Neglect 33,* 59–68.

Zahn-Waxler, C., Duggal, S. and Gruber, R. (2002) 'Parental Psychopathology.' In M. Bornstein (ed.) *Handbook of Parenting: Social Conditions and Applied Parenting,* Vol. 4. Mahwah, NJ: Erlbaum.

Ziv, Y. (2005) 'Attachment-Based Intervention Programs: Implications for Attachment Theory and Research.' In L.J. Berlin, Y. Ziv, L. Amaya-Jackson and M.T. Greenberg (eds) (2005) *Enhancing Early Attachments: Theory, Research, Intervention and Policy.* London: Guilford Press.

Subject Index

Author Index

Lightning Source UK Ltd.
Milton Keynes UK
UKOW040732220612

194833UK00001B/2/P